James Robson

The Churches and Churchyards of Berwickshire

James Robson

The Churches and Churchyards of Berwickshire

ISBN/EAN: 9783744660495

Printed in Europe, USA, Canada, Australia, Japan

Cover: Foto ©Lupo / pixelio.de

More available books at **www.hansebooks.com**

THE CHURCHES AND CHURCHYARDS OF
BERWICKSHIRE.

KELSO:
PRINTED BY RUTHERFURD & CRAIG.

THE
CHURCHES AND CHURCHYARDS

OF

BERWICKSHIRE.

BY

JAMES ROBSON,

AUTHOR OF "THE CHURCHES AND CHURCHYARDS OF ROXBURGHSHIRE,"
"BORDER BATTLES," ETC.

KELSO:
J. & J. H. RUTHERFURD, 20, SQUARE.
1893.

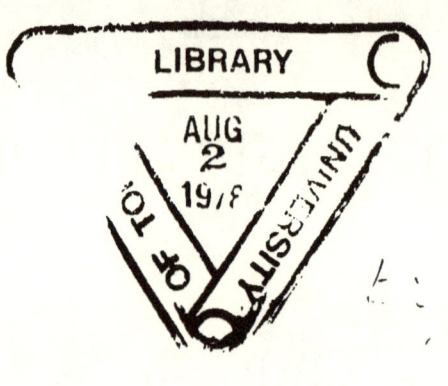

PREFACE.

TWENTY-FIVE years hence a very considerable proportion of the inscriptions and epitaphs recorded in the following pages will have entirely disappeared. This is due, not altogether—in some cases, indeed, not at all—to neglect or wilful spoliation. The laws of disintegration operate with merciless severity upon the sacred relics and the quaint and curious words engraved on their surface. Except where the stone is very durable, epitaphs, after the lapse of a couple of centuries, become defaced and unintelligible.

The memory of our forefathers, however remote the period in which they lived, however simple their lives and humble their origin, is worthy of being perpetuated. Apart altogether from the question of genealogy and pedigree, there is an element of deep pathos in all that concerns our departed kindred, and the simple words which record their virtues (not always omitting their vices). Time's stern corroding touch deals hardly with our most cherished and sacred memorials, whether in the shape of tombstones or church buildings. Sixteenth, and even seventeenth, century stones are rapidly crumbling to decay—their inscriptions, in some cases, only partially decipherable; in others so weathered as to be utterly unintelligible. It is with a view to rescue these from the oblivion which inevitably awaits them that the present work has been undertaken.

The inscriptions, with few exceptions, have been carefully copied from the stones by the author himself. This part of the work is the result of patient and laborious effort, attended, in some cases, with only partial success—words here and there being illegible.

For the general description of pre-Reformation fabrics, and especially their architectural features, the author is indebted to Mr. John Ferguson, Duns. This is given almost *verbatim et literatim* from his " Pre-Reformation Churches of Berwickshire "—a series of valuable papers which appeared in the *Berwickshire Naturalists' Club Proceedings* for 1890. To the secretary of the Club, Dr. Hardy, thanks are also due for kind permission to use these and other papers, the property of the Club.

DEANBRAE, HAWICK,
  20th June, 1896.

CONTENTS.

	Page.
ABBEY ST. BATHANS	1
AYTON	12
BUNKLE	17
PRESTON	22
CHANNELKIRK	27
CHIRNSIDE	33
COCKBURNSPATH	40
ST. HELEN'S (ALDCAMBUS)	44
COLDINGHAM	49
ST. EBBA'S	49
RENTON	64
HOUNDWOOD	64
COLDSTREAM	66
LENNEL	69
CRANSHAWS	76
DUNS	80
EARLSTON	85
ECCLES	90
BIRGHAM	95
LEITHOLM	96
MERSINGTON	96
EDROM	98
EYEMOUTH	105
FOGO	110
FOULDEN	115
GORDON	120
HUNTLEYWOOD	121
SPOTTISWOOD	121
HUME	123
GREENLAW	126
LAMBDEN	128
HALYBURTON	128
ROWESTON	128

CONTENTS.

	Page
HUTTON	131
FISHWICK	135
LADYKIRK	139
UPSETLINGTON	146
HORNDEAN	147
LANGTON	151
LAUDER	157
KEDSLIE	158
ST. LEONARD'S	158
LEGERWOOD	163
LONGFORMACUS	171
ELLEM	173
MERTOUN	175
DRYBURGH	177
MORDINGTON	187
LAMBERTON	190
NENTHORN	194
LITTLE NEWTON	197
POLWARTH	200
SWINTON	208
SIMPRIN	211
WESTRUTHER	215
BASSENDEAN	216
SPOTTISWOOD	219
WEDDERLEY	219
WHITSOME	222
HILTON	224

THE CHURCHES AND CHURCHYARDS OF BERWICKSHIRE.

Abbey St. Bathans.

THIS is one of the most ancient ecclesiastical establishments in Scotland, although, unfortunately, comparatively little is known concerning its history. That a place of such importance should have been allowed to almost entirely disappear, and all but pass from the ken of modern historians, is a proof of how much—rather, indeed, how amazingly little—interest centres around ecclesiological institutions which had their birth and flourished in ages more remote than the period of transition from Saxon to Norman dominion. An antiquity which stretches remotely back, and even invades the teens of centuries, deserves a better fate than to sink into unmerited oblivion, and fade from our mental vision as if it were but a mere fable rather than the strong and stable rock on which is reared the visible Church of God on earth.

Obscure and fragmentary as is the history of Abbey St. Bathans, we have evidence of a kind which would seem to point to the conclusion that the first religious establishment here was founded as early as the seventh century.

Like all such fabrics of that early period, it was rude, and entirely void of anything like architectural beauty. Indeed, the earliest structure here, it is believed, was simply a hut composed of wood and turf. It stood at a distance of about a quarter of a mile from the church and ancient priory of Abbey St. Bathans, and the field which contains the site has always been known as "The Chapel Field."*

No person now alive recollects the ruins. From time to time, however, in ploughing the field, stones have been turned up which apparently had formed part of the building, and thus the site of the chapel was pretty nearly ascertained, but it was only in the course of draining the field this summer (1870) that the foundations were discovered, and they have been fully traced, and are now exposed. The building is rectangular, 46 feet 6 inches in length externally, and 38 feet internally, 21 feet in breadth externally, and 15 feet 6 inches internally.

---

* It is thus spoken of in the Old Statistical Account (Sir John Sinclair's):—"About a quarter of a mile from the nunnery, on the same side of the water, lie the foundations of a small chapel and yard holding that name, but there are no marks of people having buried in it." Some time after this it seems to have fallen a prey to the vandalism of the period, and the fatal influence of the "improving laird," for in the New Statistical Account, written about fifty years later, it is stated that "these foundations have now been removed, on account of the obstruction they presented to the operations of agriculture, but the field that contained them is still called the Chapel Field."

The north wall is 3 feet thick, the east and south walls are about 3 feet 6 inches thick, and the west wall is 5 feet thick. The door has probably been in the middle of the west end, but partly from the fact that nothing except the foundations are remaining, and partly from a drain having been cut through it before the nature of the building was known, no trace of a door can now be found. In the southern half of this west end wall there is apparently a passage 1 foot 8 inches broad and about 6 feet long, entering probably from the doorway; but it is difficult to see what could be the object of it, unless it might lead to the stair of a belfry. On the south side, near the west end, is a window 3 feet 7 inches wide externally, the sides of it being formed of freestone, well, but roughly, dressed; only two courses of these stones and the window-sill remain. The sill must have been on the level of the ground. Lime has been used in the erection of this window, but it seems doubtful if the other parts of the structure have been so built. The east end has been contracted by a 2-feet wall in each corner, so as to form a small chancel 10 feet wide by 4 feet 6 inches deep. In front of this chancel is a flat gravestone 5 feet 10 inches long, 1 foot 8 inches broad at the head, or west end, and 1 foot 5 inches at the foot, or east end. A bevel of about $1\frac{1}{2}$ inches has been cut on the edges. This gravestone differs in shape from most, if not all, others in this immediate district, which are always rectangular. There is no inscription or sculpture on it. It is well dressed, but the tool-marks on it are apparently those of a pick, not of a flat chisel. In the building were found a few dressed stones for lintels, and a good many pieces of what probably has been a font about 2 feet in diameter. Some pieces of oak and large iron nails have also been found; the wood is much decayed on the outside, but the heart of it is sound and hard.*

In this parish in the year 1184, or between that and 1200, there was founded a priory or nunnery. It was dedicated to St. Mary, and founded by Ada, the liberal daughter of William the Lion, wife of Patrick Earl of Dunbar, to form a convent of Cistercian nuns. Its founders made adequate endowments of lands and revenues, besides which it received many donations from other benefactors. This nunnery, however, never reached a degree of opulence equal to those of Coldstream or Eccles, yet to be noticed. The nuns of Abbey St. Bathans appear to have had a grange at some distance from this convent, and, in the thirteenth century, they made an agreement with the prior of Coldingham to pay him twelve pennies, or a pound of pepper, yearly for their tithes of hay from a meadow at Bylie.

Ada, the prioress, and the nuns of St. Bathans swore fealty to Edward I. on 24th August, 1296, and were thereafter restored by him to their lands and rights.

After the fatal battle of Halidon Hill in 1333 the prioress and her nuns submitted to Edward, and

---

* Mr. John Turnbull, Abbey St. Bathans.—*Hist. Ber. Nat. Club*, 1870.

obtained from him, in 1334, a protection for themselves, their house, and their revenues.*

St. Bathans' priory is understood to have been originally a cell of South Berwick, but it appears at no long time after its foundation to have become independent. Remains of the conventual buildings were visible about the close of last century. The last vestiges disappeared about half a century ago.†

There is built into the front wall of the present mansion house of Abbey St. Bathans a stone bearing the following inscription:—

DVRVM PATIENTIA FRANGO 1694.

This can hardly have any, or, at all events, but a very remote, connection with the priory.‡

---

* Chalmers' *Caledonia*.

† Mr. Ferguson.—*Hist. Ber. Nat. Club*, 1890. Writing in 1860, Mr. J. C. Langlands says:—" There is scarcely anything left at Abbey St. Bathans of the ancient nunnery. Some years ago part of the doorway was to be seen within the burial ground, but all vestiges of it have been removed. A small window still remains in the eastern gable of the kirk. It has been partly walled up to hold a common window frame, above which two circular headings may be seen: these have rested in the centre on a shaft by which the window has been divided. Above them, and between them, there has been a circular opening, which is now made use of as a passage for the flue of the stove inside the kirk. The wall is very thick and much splayed, evidently showing that it has been erected outside of the wall."

‡ In the *Berwick Journal* of June 27th, 1895, Mr. R. H. Henderson, Chirnside, writes:—" To the south and east of the church of St. Bathans lay the gardens of the Priory; this spot has hence been called the Precinct Yards; around the whole was a walk of three tiers of stones, and on the east side of these gardens was another walk of considerable breadth, bearing the name of the Bishop's Loan. Why it had received this name cannot now be ascertained. It may be conjectured, however,

The present church of Abbey St. Bathans occupies a delightfully secluded position close to the right bank of the Whitadder. This was originally the church of the Priory, and was used after the Reformation. Since then the building has been so much altered and curtailed that very little of the original fabric remains. What is now the east wall —24 feet wide by 4 feet thick, and evidently for the most part ancient—is pierced about the middle of the elevation by a round-headed, widely countersplayed window—8 feet by 2 feet wide—which retains its ancient plate tracery in the head, forming a trefoiled termination to each of the two lights into which it has been divided, and displaying a quatre-foiled circle in the space above. The dividing monial is a restoration. The tracery is more worn and decayed on the internal side, and the splay of the outer sill of the window is much deeper than that of the inner one. There is also an intake on the wall above the window externally. These are somewhat puzzling features, and would seem to show that the modern church has been built to the west of the original edifice, thus converting its west wall into the eastern gable of the new structure. This view is borne out by the fact

---

that as the Priory belonged at one time to David Lindsay, son to the Archbishop of Glasgow—if this dignitary ever resided here—the Bishop's Loan may have been his favourite place of resort for walking, and there is some reason for believing that this family did at one time reside here. A stone lintel is preserved bearing the inscription *Patientia durum frango*, and as the chief of the family of Lindsay took the motto 'Endure fert,' and two of the cadets 'Patientia Vincit,' it is not improbable that this inscription may have been the motto of Prior David Lindsay."

that, close to the northern extremity of the same wall (on what is now its external side), there are stones projecting from its face as if it had extended farther to the east. The lower portion of the north wall of the church is also ancient, and near the west end may be seen traces of a blocked semi-circular-headed doorway. This, according to the writer of the New Statistical Account, communicated with the domestic buildings which stood to the north of the church, between it and the river Whitadder.*

The church has a handsome tower, and the interior, though small, is comfortable, and adorned by several windows of beautifully stained glass. The pulpit occupies the south-east corner, and near it, within a modern recess in the east wall, is a recumbent, full-length effigy of what appears to be a prioress. This interesting, and to all appearance ancient, monument had been built into the wall of the church, and during some alterations which took place a number of years ago it was removed and placed in its present position. Built into the wall of the church porch is a large stone with the following inscription :—

   " Hire . lyes . MR . George .
   Home . Minister . of . the .
   Gospel . at . Abay . St .
   Bathens . who . departed
   . this . life . the . 22 . of .
   September . 1705 . years . his .
   age. . . .
   " Hire . lyes . Iean . Hamilton
   spows . to . the . seid . Mr
   George . Home . who . de-

---

* Mr. Ferguson.—*Hist. Ber. Nat. Club*, 1890.

parted . this . life . the . 22
of . December . 1719 . and
Mortifyed . a . 1000 . Marks
for . maintaining . a . School
Master . in . this . place
her . age . 64 . years.
" Here . lyes . Ketarine . Crucks
spous . to . Ninion . Home . sone
to . the . said . Mr . George . Home."

A short distance to the east of the church is the Holy Well, or St. Bathan's Well, which bears the following beautiful inscription :—

" DEUS ADJUTORIUM
MEUM INTENDE."*

A path near this well is called " The Pilgrims' Path."

The burial ground which surrounds the church contains a few stones dating back to the seventeenth and beginning of the eighteenth centuries, though nothing very remarkable in the way of inscriptions. On a small stone are these words—

" Here lyes Elisabeth Smitton daughter of Walter Smitton who departed this life in the 1 day of Agust 1731."

A medium-sized stone, though comparatively

---

* According to the superstition of ancient times, this spring had the power of healing diseases, and its waters, as is still the belief of the neighbourhood, neither fog nor freeze : they even prevent a mill-lade into which they flow from being locked up in winter with ice. A dramatic writer, little known to fame, takes a simile from this circumstance, making one of his characters praise the wit of another as pure, and never failing, by saying —

" The wit is like St. Bathan's crystal well,
That never fogs or freezes, always pure."

—Mr R. H. Henderson.—*Berwick Journal*, 27th June, 1895.

modern, is curiously inscribed in very rude lettering thus—

"Here lyes Thomas Miller who died in Desmbr 6th 1778 aged 77 years as also hise spoues Isbel Trotter who died in dsmbr 24th 1763 aged 85 years as also there sone who died jenry 24 1762 aged 19 years."

The inscription on a very plain stone, which is the oldest decipherable, reads thus:—

"Here lyes Patrick Iohnston uho departed this life the 1 day of May 1698 and of his age 45.

"Here lyes Iean Moffat spous to Patrick Iohnston uho departed this life the 11 of April 1723 and of her age 76.

"Here lyes Margret Coun spous to Iames Iohnston uho departed this life the 27 of September 1723 & of her age 42."

The following appears on an exceedingly small stone:—

"Tod who departed this life the 2 daie of Aprill 1718 and of her age 72 years."

About a mile west of the priory, at Strafontain (Trefontanis), there was another nunnery and chapel, which was also a cell of Berwick. It was founded by David I. in 1118. It seems to have been suppressed in the beginning of the fifteenth century, and in 1450 the lands were given to the Collegiate Church of Dunglass, to which the church, with a hospital attached to it, was annexed as a prebend.*

In 1437 there was a "Donatio ecclesiæ, sen hospitalis de Lamyria," by John, abbot of Alnwick, to John de Coldstream and the other monks of Dryburgh, which hospital seems to have been

---

* Mr. Ferguson.—*Hist. Ber. Nat. Club*, 1890.

delivered to their charge in the year 1436 by Henry, the bishop of St. Andrews.*

Alas! alas! church, nunnery, hospital, and burial ground have all disappeared. Not a vestige now remains to remind us of former greatness. Portions of the church and burial ground were visible at the end of last century, but were totally removed some years later.

Something of the state of the separate churches in this parish may be gathered from the following report:—" The estait of the Kirkis of St. Bothanes and Strafontanes with the value of the teyndis gewing vpe be James Stevinsone and Alexander Robesone the 18 of Junii 1627. Communicants ane hundreth and fortie. The farthest pairt from the kirk is not two full myles.

"The kirkis since the reformatioun hes ever bene conjoynit and vnder ane ministrie.

"The kirkis are not of one qualitie not haveing one patrone.

"The Kirk of St. Bothanes within the precinct of the monasterie of old for nunes hes the kingis Maiestie for patron. The Kirk of Strafontanes the Erle Hume it being a pendicle of the colledge Kirk of Dunglas."†

The following is a list of the ministers that have been in Abbey St. Bathans since 1591 :—

Matthew Liddell—1591 to 1608.
George Reidpath, M.A.—1627 to 1628.

---

* Sir Lewis Stewart's MS. Col. No. 2.
† Reports of the state of certain parishes in Scotland, from the originals, preserved in General Register House.

ABBEY ST. BATHANS.

Thomas Suyntoune, M.A.—1628 to 1649.
George Pollok, M.A.—1650 to 1663.
James Cokburne, M.A.—1664 to 1674.
James Dunbar, M.A.—1675 to 1681.
Robert Bowmaker, M.A.—1682 to 1697.
George Hume, M.A.—1699 to 1705.
George Hume, of Abbey, M.A.—1707 to 1718.
James Hall, M.A.—1719 to 1754.*
Alexander Hume—1755 to 1758.
Adam Murray—1759 to 1774.
John Sked—1774 to 1810.
Alexander Anderson—1813 to 1822.
John Wallace—1823 to 1843.†
Thomas Davidson—1843 to 1873.
Peter Christie (present incumbent)—1873.

---

* Hall was suspended for having a penny wedding in his house, which gave great scandal to the neighbourhood!—Scott's *Fasti Ecclesiæ Scoticanæ.*

† Wallace, on adhering to the Protest, joining in the Free Secession, and signing the Deed of Demission, was declared no longer a minister of this church, 24th May, 1843. He was the last member of the Assembly who left the venerable house on that memorable departure.—Scott's *Fasti Ecclesiæ Scoticanæ.*

Ayton.

THE church of Ayton is supposed to date back to a period not later than the close—more probably the middle—of the twelfth century. It was granted by the Scottish Edgar to St. Cuthbert's monks, and thus became the property of the priory of Coldingham, of which it was a subordinate cell, and remained such till the Reformation. It was dedicated to St. Dionysius. In the year 1380 the church was the scene of an important historical event. John of Gaunt, in this year, met the Scottish commissioners whom King Robert II. had appointed to arrange for a renewal of the truce between the two countries; and a similar meeting was held in the church in 1384. Then on 30th September, 1497, a truce was entered into between England and Scotland to last for seven years. It was signed in the church of Ayton, on behalf of King James, by Andrew Forman, &c., &c.

Amongst the earlier chaplains—he was probably the first—connected with this church was *Robertus Parsona Capellae de Ayton*, the date of whose tenure of office is somewhat indefinite, but was between the years 1166 and 1232.

The original building stood in the churchyard, and was built in the form of a St. John's cross. The foundations of that part of its walls which constituted the nave, as also the eastern wall of the chancel and a considerable portion of the south transept, constructed of square hewn sandstone, remained undisturbed, and formed part of the successor of the original church. The whole fabric is now roofless, but forms a picturesque ruin.

The old belfry stands almost complete, clothed with a thick mantle of ivy, while the side walls are in some parts fairly entire. The south transept of this original church has been used for many years as the private burial vault of the Fordyce family, formerly proprietors of Ayton Castle. The window in this part is worthy of special notice. It affords an excellent specimen of the intermixture between the Saxon and Norman styles of architecture, as seen from its circular arch and massive mullions—a style which was introduced into Scotland during the twelfth century. Grave doubts, however, are entertained as to the antiquity of this part of the old building. After a very careful and minute examination of the place a few years ago, Mr. Ferguson writes:—"If the adjunct called the south transept has not been a late addition to the church, the window has been a late insertion in the transept. It is round headed, no doubt, but is of much larger dimensions than the ordinary type of Norman window, and is divided into three lights by mullions crossed by a transom bar. The tracery is still entire, and is of the most ungainly description, looking more like the debased work of the seventeenth or eighteenth centuries than that of any of the mediæval styles. Of course, the fact of its being bar tracery conclusively shows that it is long posterior to the Norman period; and it is impossible to avoid the suspicion that it may have been one of the 'improvements' referred to in the Old Statistical

Account as having been made upon the church not many years before it was written. The east wall of the church was nearly entire about half-a-century ago, but has since been removed, so that the dimensions of that portion of the building cannot now be ascertained. The nave has been about 75 feet long by 20 feet 6 inches wide, but none of its original features are now visible. The belfry tower on the north side was a late addition.*

Near the village of Ayton is a holy well, still in use, which was dedicated to St. Ebba.

One communion cup of considerable antiquity is engraved—"This cup originally given by Magdallan Rule of Peelwalls to the Church of Ayton in 1677. Renewed and enlarged in 1780." Another cup is engraved—" The Parish Church of Ayton 1780."

The present church is a handsome structure, and was erected in 1865, in the Gothic style of architecture. It is cruciform—one transept complete, apse, and cloister. It contains a handsome rose window and an elegant spire 130 feet high.

The churchyard is large, and contains many tombstones of varying form and size, some of which date 250 years back. An exceedingly small stone bears date only—1648.

A large horizontal stone has the following interesting inscription :—

"Patrick Home of Bastilridge deceast in the year 1657 aged 48.

" Heir lyes William Home of Bastelrige his son who deceast Agust 3 1693 aged 54."

* *Hist. Ber. Nat. Club*, 1890.

A large stone bears the following beautiful lines:—

"Though distant climes divide us here below,
Though far apart we moulder into dust,
Hope says, and gently dries the tears of woe,
You all shall meet to mingle with the blest."

A neat little stone is inscribed thus, and is interesting on account of the strange and incongruous mixture of small and capital letters:—

"HErE LIES ThE BOdY
OF GOrGE BrUN WhO
DeID ThIS LIFE JUIY
ANE 1729 ANd OF
MarGrET hOG HIS
SPOUS WhO DYd NEVMBrE
8 1725."

The following words appear on a very small stone:—

"Here lyes the corps of Gelbert Hoog who departed this life decmber the 28 day 1736 his age 80 years. Illen Allanshaw who died December 20 day 1724.

A large aisle surrounded by a strong wall contains the tombs of the ancestors of the Hoods of Stainrig. In the interior was inserted a tablet with the following:—

OLIM SIC ERAT.

"This aisle was built and the tombstones repaired by John Hood of Stoneridge. A.D. 1830."

The inscription on one of the stones repaired runs thus:—

"Here lyeth the corpse of Thomas Hwde born 1648 Departed this lyffe 1697

"His father James Hwde sold ye land of Hoodsland in Aymouth parish which belonged to his predecessor."

There is also the large family burying ground of

the Inneses of Ayton Castle (the place has been sold by them quite recently). It is enclosed by a high and massive iron railing.

The family of Fordyce, formerly proprietors of Ayton Castle, have also a private burying vault here formed of the interior of the south transept of the original church. A marble tablet in the interior is thus inscribed:—

"In memory of the Right Hon'ble John Fordyce, M.P., of Ayton. Many years Receiver-General for Scotland and Commissioner of Woods and Forests under the Right Hon'ble William Pitt. He died in London, 1st July, 1809.

"Also of Katherine, his wife, daughter of Sir William Maxwell, 3d Bart. of Monreith. She died 6th March, 1815."

The names of the ministers that have been in Ayton since 1585 are as follows:—

Robert Hislop—1585 to 1586.
John Home—1586 to 1601.
William Hog—1601 to 1616.
Alexander Home—1617 to 1626.
George Home, M.A.—1627 to 1650.
Alexander Gibsone, M.A.—1652 to 1652 (a few months).
William Hume—1653 to 1664.
John Bethune, M.A.—1667 to 1689.
George Hume, M.A.—1694 to 1706.
Thomas Anderson—1712 to 1751.
Patrick Hepburn—1753 to 1772.
George Home—1773 to 1816.
Abraham Home (assistant and successor)—1799 to 1814.
George Tough (assistant and successor)—1814 to 1842.
Daniel Cameron—1843 to 1882.
J. J. Marshall Lang Aiken, B.D. (present incumbent)—1882.

There is a United Presbyterian Church at Ayton, originally built in 1776 and rebuilt in 1872. It is an elegant Gothic structure, with tall spire. The present minister is William Wilson, settled in 1869.

Bunkle and Preston.

These were separate parishes up till the latter end of the sixteenth century, when they were united, and formed into one parish under the name of Bunkle.

The original church of Bunkle is ancient, as, in connection with the parish boundaries, David I. had to settle a controversy about the proper limits of "Bonkillscire and Coldinghamscire" (*scire* is here used in the sense of parish), and William the Lion was called on to settle the same boundaries by pertinacious parties.*

Of the original structure nothing remains but the small semicircular Norman apse, which stands a short distance to the south-east of the modern building. This is probably one of the earliest examples of mediæval ecclesiastical architecture in Scotland. Mr. Muir, no mean authority, believes that it may date from even before the beginning of the 12th century; and the excessive plainness—I had almost said rudeness—of such features as it presents certainly indicates great antiquity. The arch which opened to the chancel is totally devoid of ornament, being a plain semi-circular-headed, square-edged specimen, resting on slightly

---

* Chalmers' *Caledonia*.

projecting imposts (7 feet 4 inches above the level of the ground), square on the upper edge, but chamfered on the lower. The north-west corner has evidently been repaired at a very recent date, and two stones built into it, which were doubtless taken from some other part of the ancient church, are marked with the zig-zag or chevron ornament in its earliest and simplest form. On several stones in the facing of the west wall, and on some of the voussoirs of the arch, a variety of masons' marks are observable—some of them similar to those on the earliest Norman portions of Jedburgh Abbey. The walls of the apse are 3 feet in thickness. The roof is a plain rounded vault internally, and is covered on the outside with stone slabs. A slightly projecting cornice, with a hollow chamfer below, runs along the top of the wall; and there is a narrow basement course, with a plain slope above, close to the ground. The only window is a small round-headed one, which looks to the south-east, slightly bevelled round the outer edge, and very widely splayed within. The orientation is nearly due east.*

Only very recently there have been discovered traces of what has evidently been another window similar to the round-headed one already described. It is at the opposite side of the structure, and looks towards the north-east. A rectangular piscina niche, a little below and to the right of this window, which was built up and concealed from view in 1890, has been recently revealed by the

---

* Mr. Ferguson.—*Hist. Ber. Nat. Club.*

decayed state of the plaster, and is now exposed in its original state.*

---

* In this apse lie the remains of the murdered Mrs. Margaret Home.

"NORMAN ROSS.

"The lady's gane, and Norman's ta'en,
  Norman wi' the bloody hand ;
Now he will hae to pay the kain
  For being at the deil's command.

"Norman Ross, wi' pykit pow,
  Three corbies at his e'en ;
Girnin' in the gallows tow,
  Sic a sight was never seen."

Norman Ross, to whom the above rhyme refers, was a confidential servant to Mrs. Margaret Home, Lady Billy, widow of Mr. Ninion Home of Billy, in the parish of Buncle, in the year 1751. Lady Billy then resided at Linthill, an old mansion near Eyemouth ; and on Monday evening, the 12th of August, Norman Ross concealed himself in his mistress's room while she was out enjoying a walk ; and after she had come in, and gone to bed, Norman, supposing her asleep, came forth from his hiding place, and attempting to take her pocket with her keys from under her pillow, in order to get at her money, the lady awoke, and Norman immediately ran to the drawers which stood in the room, and, seizing a case knife lying on the top of them, therewith cut her throat across ; and as she resisted by grasping at his hair, and making other efforts for life, she was sadly mangled with the knife, in her hands, arms, and other parts of her body. The noise occasioned by the struggle having awoke the servants below, one of them ran directly upstairs, and saw the ruffian returning out of the lady's room, and immediately after he went out at a window. He was taken next day in a field of corn near the house, being unable to escape to any distance in consequence, it is said, of having broken a leg in his descent from the window, and was carried by a party of military to the gaol at Greenlaw. The unfortunate lady died on Friday the 16th of August, 1751, the fourth day after she received her wounds. Norman Ross was tried for the murder before the High Court of Justiciary at Edinburgh, on the 11th November following, and was found guilty of the crime libelled. He was sentenced to be executed

The church was repaired about 1718, and a century later the original building was almost completely demolished—only the Norman apse left, as already observed—and the materials used for the erection of the present church in 1820.

From the following extract we get some idea of the ecclesiastical condition of the parish in the early part of the seventeenth century:—

"The valuation of the landes and teindis and kirk landis within the parische and barony of Bonckell.

"Imprimis, thair be fyfe hundredth communicantis in the parochin. Item, the extent of the parochin is three myllis in lenth and three in bread; the kirk standis in the midis of the parochin. The furdest house in the parochin is not twa myllis ffrom the kirk. The kirk of Prestone is vnyted to the kirk off Bonckell. It was vnyted be the direction off the last Parliament holdin at Edinburch be our gracious soverane off worthie memori King James [the Sext], and be the plate ordeaned to be haldin ffor the provisione off kirkis vnprovydid, as Bonckell was at that tyme. And the furthest house off the parochin of Prestone is nocht twa myllis ffrom the kirk of Bonckell: The Resones off the vnion. Both the parochins wer on lordis land or Barronj; the kirk of Bonckell in the midis off the Barronj. Both the parochines but fyf hundreth communicantes: the case off thes kirks befoir the vnion was. In the

---

at the Gallowlee, between Edinburgh and Leith. The narrative states that the mourners had proceeded for a considerable distance before any one discovered that they had left Linthill without the corpse of the murdered lady!—*The Popular Rhymes, Sayings, and Proverbs of the County of Berwick*, by George Henderson, surgeon, Chirnside.

paroch of Prestone twa hundreth communicantes. The stipend of the Minister of Bonckell then threscoir pundis money, and the viccarage estimat abone the worth to twa hundreth merkes, but then nocht worth ane hundreth pundis with manse and glib. The Minister at Prestone then fyftie pund, and the wiccarage reakinet to ane hundreth mairkis, but abone the worth nocht worth fyftie poundes, with his manse and gleib and pertinentis. It is the bischop of Dunkell his propper kirk. The Bischop is persone of both thes parochines. The viccaragis of both the parochinis are at the Bischopis gift.

    (Signed)   "Dauid Lumisden
         off Blanerne,
       Adame Trumbill,
       J. Gaittis, minister at
        Bonckell.

"At Bonckell Kirk the first
 of Junij, 1627."

A reaction seems to have set in in regard to these two previously separate churches, and a desire for their disunion. "The Brethrein of the presbitrie considdering the estait of thir tua kirkis that hea bein tua several parochinnis befor the reformation, and sensyne served with twa severall ministers with manssis and gleibis, and provision for the tyme, maist humblie we intreat your L. to disioyne the samyn in respect thair is sufficient maintenance for the provision of them both be the teyndis greit and small, and sufficient flockis for them both, as also thair is ane great hart burning betuix thir tua parochinnis, and dois not resort to the heiring of the vord as it becommis good peopill, and this to be done without prejudice of the present minister's stipend.

"Sic subscribitur;

"Mr. J. Methuen, minister of Fogo.

"Mr. Jhone Weemse, minister at Dunse."

&c., &c., &c.*

Bunkle Church, erected in 1820, is a plain, rectangular, barn-like structure, so plain indeed that, but for the belfry, one would scarcely suspect it was a church at all. Surrounding it is the churchyard, which contains nothing of interest. The oldest stone with legible inscription bears the following:—

"Here lyes the corps of Thomas Atchison, who died Jan. 1, 1686."

The communion plate consists of two cups, which are thus inscribed:—

"For the use of the United Parishes of Bunkle and Prieston, 26 Feby., 1755."

The ruins of PRESTON CHURCH and the old burial ground occupy an elevated position on the left bank of the Whitadder, about a mile and a half from Bunkle.

The existing ruins of the old pre-Reformation Church of Preston are sufficient to enable us to form a tolerably accurate idea of its form and dimensions. Like nearly all the old churches, it was long and very narrow; the length being about

---

* *Reports on the State of Certain Parishes in Scotland.*

three times its width. The main building consisted of a nave and chancel. The wall on the north side of the nave is entirely demolished, while considerable portions on the south remain; and the west gable is pretty entire. On the north side of the building there are obscure indications of a lateral adjunct, which Mr. Ferguson suggests may have been a sacristy.

The chancel, which measures internally 18 feet 6 inches by 14 feet 6 inches, is much less ruinous than the nave, but is so overgrown with ivy that its features are barely discernible. In the east gable are two obtusely-pointed windows, 4 feet 10 inches apart, each $3\frac{1}{2}$ feet high by 1 foot 3 inches wide. On the outside they are flush with the wall, the edges being merely chamfered, and each of the pointed heads is cut out of one stone. Internally, they are widely splayed, with a segmental arch above. There is a smaller window in the south wall, very obtusely pointed outside, but having a flat head and sill within. Underneath it is a piscina of very poor and rude character, but interesting as the only example *in situ* left in Berwickshire, if we except those in Dryburgh Abbey. It has an excessively shallow basin sunk in a square stone, which is inserted diagonally in the wall, so as to leave a triangular projection of about 18 inches at the base of an equally shallow round-headed recess, measuring 2 feet 2 inches by 1 foot 6 inches. The basin stone is corbelled off below, and has a plain half-round moulding along the under edge, and running up the front angle of the projecting portion. In the west wall of the chancel there is observable a blocked semi-circular arch, which may have been the original chancel arch, although the dressing of the stones on the side next the nave has a suspiciously modern look. The only feature in the west gable of the nave is a blocked pointed window, closely resembling those in the east gable, but a little wider and scarcely so high. The church, as at first built, was entered by two square-headed, plainly chamfer-edged doorways in the south wall, one opening into the nave and the other into the chancel. A third at the east end of the nave has been added at a comparatively recent period. In the wall, immediately above this last-mentioned doorway, there is inserted a circular stone, $12\frac{1}{2}$ inches in diameter, with a cross *patée* carved in high relief upon it. This can hardly have been a consecration cross, these being usually incised or cut in low-relief. Whatever may have been its original significance or use, it has, no doubt, been placed in its present position at the time of the construction of the doorway just referred to.*

Adjacent to the church on the south side is the churchyard, still used for interments in the southern part of the parish.

An old weather-worn stone, with some exquisite carved work on it, bears date 1672, with death's-head, cross bones, &c.

A small, very plain stone is inscribed:—

"Here lyes the body of Jeams Cowen died 27 January 1711 his eag 67 years."

---

* Mr. Ferguson.—*Hist. Ber. Nat. Club*, 1890.

On a neat slate-coloured stone, erected to the memory of a husband and wife, are these lines:—

> "Cease then frail nature to lament in vain,
> Reason forbids to wish them back again;
> Rather congratulate their happy fate,
> And their advancement to a glorious state."

The old communion tokens, which were struck in 1790, are still preserved, and are of three different kinds.

First, the square ones, inscribed on one side thus:—

"Buncle & Preston."

On the other side:—

"M$\underline{r}$ R . D 1790."

These are the initials of Robert Douglas, minister (see list of ministers).

Second, the round ones, inscribed:—

"$\frac{B}{P}$ K"

on one side; the reverse side is plain.

Third, round, and inscribed:—

"B P"

The following is a list of the ministers that have been in Bunkle since 1582:—

William Sinclair—1582 to 1599.
George Reidpath, M.A.—1599 to 1607.
Matthew Carrail—1607 to 1612.
John Gaittis*—1614 to 1640.

---

* Gaittis, being at the castle of Dunglass with a party of soldiers, left to watch the motions of the garrison of Berwick, under the command of Thomas Earl of Haddington, the powder magazine was fired by an incendiary, and exploded, 30th August, 1640, when the commander, Mr. G., and about sixty-six others, were killed, while thirty-three were wounded.—Scott's *Fasti Ecclesiæ Scoticanæ.*

Robert Colden, M.A.—1650 to 1664.
George Trotter, M.A.—1665 to 1677.
Alexander Nicolson, M.A.—1678 to 1689.
Alexander Colden, M.A.—1690 to 1693.
Ninian Home, M.A.—1696 to 1704.
Walter Hart, M.A.—1706 to 1761.
Robert Douglas—1765 to 1801.
John Campbell—1802 to 1818.
Archibald M'Conechy*—1819 to 1843.
John Dunlop—1843 to 1880.
Ludovic Mair (present incumbent)—1880.

PRESTON.

William Sinclair—1590 to 1616.

---

* M'Conechy, on joining in the Free Secession and signing the Deed of Demission, was declared no longer a minister of this church, 20th June, 1843.—Scott's *Fasti Ecclesiæ Scoticanæ.*

Channelkirk.

THE name was written in the parish records in 1650 *Chingalkirk.**
A church existed here in the time of David I. (1124–1153). By a grant of that king, Hugh Morville became proprietor of the district and the advowson of the ancient church. Subsequently, Morville, in gratitude to his royal benefactor, as much as from motives of piety, soon after gifted the church to the canons of Dryburgh. This gift was confirmed by his son, Richard Morville, after the death of Hugh in 1162, and was approved by Malcolm IV. (1153–1165). The church remained in possession of the canons of Dryburgh till the Reformation. It was dedicated to St. Cuthbert, who once lived in this part, and, according to the story of his life, as a boy he lived here "under the care of a certain religious man" during the absence of his mother on a pilgrimage to Rome. Mention is also made in the anonymous Life of St. Cuthbert that "he was watching over the flocks of his master near the river Leader," and it was here that he had that vision which led him to devote himself to a religious life, and forthwith he became a monk in the monastery of Melrose.

The original church was cruciform in shape. In

---

* It has been contended, though on very slender authority, that the ancient name was *Children's Kirk*, because it was dedicated to the children of Bethlehem, or the Holy Innocents.

1627 the building was in a partially ruinous condition. According to an official report of that year "the quir was without ane roofe, to the great scandall off the gospell and prejudice of the parishiners." In 1702 it underwent extensive alterations and repairs, and in 1817 the old walls were taken down and the present building erected in its stead. We learn something of the state of this church and parish in the year 1627 from an official report issued that year:—

"Parish of Chingilkirk.

"For the church of Chingilkirk, quhilk holdis of Drybrughe.

"Thair hes nott beine as yitt a manse for a minister by reasone of the none residence of my predecessours, so that I am very ewill vsit.

"I have no sowmes grasse nor muire to cast elding and diffott into, to my great hurt and skaith, notwithstanding thair is muche kirkland in my parochine, as Over Howden, Nether Howden, twa husband landis in Huxtoune, and my Lady Ormeistoune's kirklandis besyde the kirk, and the Hillhouse, quhilk perteines to the Laird of Herdmeistoune.

"It is shame to sie the queir so long without ane roofe, neither can the parochiners gett halfe rowme in the kirk.

"The quir is without ane roofe, to the great scandall of the gospell and prejuduce of the parishiners that cannot get rowme in the kirk, the quir being doune.

"It is not fewd land, but being viccars land of

old, and now withholden from the ministery at that kirk, hinders satling, and maid all my predecessouris non-residentis; neither can I get grasse to two kye, to my great greiffe and skaith, quhilk I hope shall now be gratiouslie amendid, to the perpetuall satling of a ministry at that kirk.

"If it shall please the Lord to withhold His judgments from the land, so that thir fore-namitt rowmes be weill plenishit they may yeild the forsaid stok and teind, and quhen the ground is punishit, the heritour and teinder must nott be frie.

"Thus have I *(bona fide)* vsit all diligence to informe myself anent the premisses, neither might I opinlie tak the help of my parishiners, because being maillmen and in wsse to pay for the teindis they wald have sett all things at naught, quhilk I could not suffer, and thairfoir hes takin the wholle burtheine on myself, and yit hes neither prejudgit maister nor tennand. In the meane tyme, but keiping ane pure conscience, hes indevoirit to give all possible satisfactioune to all parties that hes any interest in this business, and that indifferently, without any partiall deilling.

"Mr. Henry Cokburne,
Minister of the Evangell
off our Lord att Chingilkirke."

The church occupies a commanding position, and, with the hamlet of Channelkirk, is said to stand within the area of an old Roman camp. The building, with the exception of its crow-stepped gables and projecting cornice below, is severely plain. The interior is exceedingly comfortable, having been recently renovated.

The churchyard surrounding the church contains one or two interesting stones.

A peculiarly-shaped stone, with several rudely-carved, grotesque human figures, is thus inscribed:—

"Heir lieth Marion Brock daughter to William Brock Gardinr in Wxton [?] who deperted the 29 of Aprile 1721 and of hir age 19 years."

Below this are rudely carved the rake, spade, and cross bones.

On a very small stone are these words:—

"Here lyes my bones
Now fred from groanes
Waiting the spring.
"My saul's above
With Christ in love
And there doth ring."

On the other side of this stone we read:—

"Here lyes John Dewar Husband to Elspeth Stevart who departed this life the 24 of March 1685 being the 65 year of hir age."

A very large horizontal stone is thus inscribed along the bevelled edges:—

"Omnem diem tibi defluxisse supremum."

And on the flat upper surface:—

"Here lyes the body of William Wigrt tenant in Glengelt who died Apr 16 1682."

In early times there were two chapels in this parish subordinate to the church of Channelkirk—one at Glengelt and the other at Confrac.

Concerning the chapel of Glengelt, it is stated that "Henry de Murdeville," who enjoyed the lands of Glengelt in the reign of William the Lion (1165-1214), granted to the canons of Dryburgh an indemnity that the chapel of Glengelt should not injuriously affect the mother church of "Childin-kirk."*

Of the chapel at Confrae, it is recorded that, in the thirteenth century, John de St. Clair, who possessed the lands of Carfrae, granted an indemnity to the canons of Dryburgh that his chapel of Confrae should not injure the mother church of Childinkirk.†

Of these chapels not a vestige now remains.

A quarter of a mile to the west there is a perennial spring of excellent water called the Well of the Holy Water Cleugh—a name conferred by ancient superstition.

A road, called the Girthgate, passing through the western boundary of the parish, was used by the monks on their way from Melrose to Edinburgh. It is a broad green path, on which, it is said, the surrounding heath never grows. On this road, a few miles due west of the church, were to be seen, not many years ago, the ruins of an old building commonly known by the name of Rest Law, or Restlaw Haw. Tradition tells us that this was the place where monks and pilgrims stopped or rested for refreshment, it being about half-way between Melrose and Edinburgh.‡

The following is a list of the ministers that have been in Channelkirk since 1611:—

John Gibsoun, reader in Channelkirk—1576.
Allan Lundie, M.A.—1611 to 1614.

---

* *Chartulary of Dryburgh.*
† *Chartulary of Dryburgh.*
‡ *Old Statistical Account.*

Francis Collace, M.A.—1615 to 1625.
Henry Cockburn, M.A.—1625 to 1650.
David Liddell, M.A.—1654 to 1662.
Henry Cockburn, M.A. (reinstated)—1662 to 1663.
Walter Keyth, M.A.—1663 to 1682.
William Arrott, M.A.—1683 to 1696.
Henry Home, M.A.—1702 to 1751.
David Scott—1752 to 1792.
Thomas Murray—1793 to 1808.
John Brown—1809 to 1828.
James Rutherford—1828 to 1862.
James Walker—1862 to 1884.
Joseph Lowe—1885 to 1891.
Archibald Allan, M.A. (present incumbent)—1892.

Chirnside.

OF the early history and date of foundation of the original church of Chirnside we know very little, beyond the fact that it is very ancient. It has been asserted, indeed, though with insufficient evidence, that a temple or place of worship existed here previous to the eleventh century, and was used by the aboriginal inhabitants. Certain it is that a church and place of defence were erected at Chirnside at a very early period. The church and its pertinents were granted by the Scottish Edgar (1097–1107) to the monks of Coldingham; so that at that early period, if not before, a church existed here. There is a tradition in the district that the western door, which is part of the original structure, is as old as the Saxon heptarchy. Unfortunately, however, there is no evidence whatever to support this theory.

The church in the thirteenth century was a rectory in the deanery of the Merse. The first of its clergy on record is Symon, *parsona de Chirnesyde*, who flourished between the years 1248 and 1249. The patronage of the rectory of Chirnside anciently belonged to the Earls of Dunbar, and when Earl Patrick founded the collegiate church of Dunbar, during the reign of David II., he annexed to it the advowson and property of the church, which thus formed one of the collegiate prepends. William de Blida (Blythe), successor to Symon above mentioned, swore fealty to Edward I. in August, 1296, and in consequence had his forfeited property restored.

The church formerly possessed the adjunct of a western tower, which was taken down about the year 1750; and it would seem, from a reference in the Old Statistical Account of the parish, to have been vaulted in stone. The existing south wall, and portions of the others, are of great thickness, and are probably original; but if so, they have been to a considerable extent refaced in the course of the somewhat frequent repairs and restorations to which the building has been subjected. It is fortunate that these operations—the last of which was carried through in 1876, and in a manner, let us thankfully admit, on the whole, both tasteful and appropriate—have left to us in very nearly its original state the interesting doorway already referred to. It consists of a recessed semi-circular archway of two square-edged orders, rising from cylindrical shafts, with scolloped capitals and square abaci, the lower edges of which are bevelled off. The daylight, or actual entrance to the building, is square headed, with a flattish edge roll round the jambs and lintel; and the tympanum, which measures 18 inches to the soffit of the inner arch, is quite plain. The outer face of the inner order is chevroned; two quarter rolls, placed side by side, are carried round the external one; and a plain weather moulding or hood, sloping on the upper side, but square below, surmounts the whole. All the mouldings, except the chevron, are sadly mutilated and wasted. The two outer pillars, with the exception of their capitals and abaci, are restorations, as are also the bases of the inner ones, and it is to be regretted that the mistake has been committed of making each of the restored shafts a disengaged monolith, whereas in the old work they were cut out of the jambs. The doorway is placed within a broad shallow quasi porch, near the west end of the south wall, and projecting about ten inches from the wall face.*

Near the old doorway may be seen a fragment of what formed a necessary factor for disciplinary purposes in every church edifice—viz., the *jougs*. Only a few links remain of this relic of a barbarous custom. This instrument was used as a sort of pillory for a certain class of delinquents, such as those who were guilty of too vigorous scolding, brawling, fighting, swearing, drunkenness, &c.

On the south-west corner of the church is an old sundial, which bears the motto:—

"*Hog aye dam lumen adest*, 1816."†

The building itself is a long, low structure, with no pretensions to grandeur of design or architectural style. The church was rebuilt in 1572, since

---

* Mr. Ferguson.—*Hist. Ber. Nat. Club*, 1890.

† The dial itself is older than the lettering. The church dates from the Norman period, and some work of that time is still left; but it has undergone many transformations and repairs, and on the north gable there is a stone inscribed, "Repaired 1705." This is a much likelier date for the dial than 1816, the date it bears. Dr. Stuart, Chirnside, states that there are several old dials in the village, and that a man named Dunbar was in old times in the habit of making them.—Macgibbon & Ross' *Castellated and Domestic Architecture of Scotland*.

which time it has undergone several alterations and repairs.

The interior of the church is neat, and, by means of the improvements effected in the renovation and repairs in 1876, is exceedingly comfortable. Inserted in the wall, to the right of the pulpit, is a stone, inscribed in rude lettering, thus:—

<blockquote>"Helpe the Pvr   1573   V E."</blockquote>

In the Old Statistical Account it is stated that this stone was taken down at the rebuilding of the east aisle or old choir, but the date of these operations is not given.

Prominent amongst the stones in the churchyard are those erected to the memory of the famous Erskines. On a small, but neat, stone are these words:—

"Young Henry Areskines corps lyes here (O ! stone . keep . in . record . his . dust . with . thee . his . soule . above . we . hope . is . with . the . lord) who departed this life July 9 1696 of his age 90."

On the other side of this stone are the hour glass and (much defaced) the words "*Memento mori.*"

Near by, on a large horizontal stone, is a Latin inscription, stating that Erskine was minister of Chirnside, and the date of his death, with a fine eulogy of his character and virtues:—

<blockquote>"M   S</blockquote>

"Mri Hen: Areskini pastoris Chirnsidis qui objit 10 Aug. 1696 ætatis suæ 72 sanctus Areskinus saxo qui conditur isto est Lapis æterni vious in Aede Dei non astu Lapis his technave volubilis ulla quippe fide in petra constabilitus erat.

(Under this stone there lyes a stone Living with God above Built on the Rock was such an one whom force nor Fraud could move.)

CHIRNSIDE.

A handsome monument is also erected to his memory, and bears the following inscription :—

"Erected by Subscription. 1825.

"In memory of the Reverend Henry Erskine, a descendant of the family of Mar, and some time Minister of this Parish, who was eminently distinguished by his Incorruptible Integrity in private life, Undaunted Zeal in the service of his Heavenly Master, and steady attachment to the Religious Principles of the Church of Scotland, at a time when the profession of these principles often led to imprisonment and exile, both of which he himself endured with exemplary resignation and fortitude. He was born at Dryburgh, in the year 1624, ordained at Cornhill in 1649, Ejected in 1662, and persecuted for nonconformity to Prelacy; admitted, soon after the revolution in 1688, to be Minister of Chirnside, where he continued in the Faithful Discharge of his Pastoral Duties till 10th August, 1696, when his holy and exemplary life terminated in a peaceful and triumphant death in the 72d year of his age and 47th of his Ministry.

"His two younger sons, Ebenezer and Ralph Erskine, were the Founders of the Secession Church."

A small stone bears the words:—

"Robert Darling.
1690."

The following interesting inscription appears on a large horizontal stone with bevelled edges:—

"Here lys the corps of Richard Spenc son to Iames Spenc of Spenc Smains who departed this life the 20 of Ianu 1685 and his age 19 years.

"And Iames Spenc Lard of Spenc Smains ther father who departed this life the 10 of Ianu 1699 and his age 66 years and Dauid Spenc son to the deceast Iames Spenc of Spenc Smains who departed this life.

[Left margin:] "And Christian Broun spoues to deceast Iames Spenc of Spenc Smains who died the 20 of Agust 1629 and of heer age 68 years."

[Right margin:] "10 of June 1699 and Agnes Spenc and of his age 29 years."

The following is a list of the ministers that have been in Chirnside since 1578:—

    Thomas Storie—1578 to 1585.
    —— Cranstoun—1585 to 1590.
    David Home, M.A.—1593 to 1606.
    Alexander Smyth—1607 to 1645.
    Patrick Smith, M.A.—1645 to 1649.
    William Galbraith, M.A.—1659 to 1669.
    James Lawtie—1669 to 1689.
    Henry Areskine, M.A.—1690 to 1696.
    William Miller, M.A.—1699 to 1702.
    George Home—1704 to 1755.
    Abraham Home (assistant)—1741 to 1748.
    Walter Anderson, M.A.—1756 to 1800.
    Thomas Logan, M.D.—1801 to 1838.
    James Wilson—1838 to 1870.
    Alexander Forteath Smart (present incumbent)—1870.

In the centre of the village of Chirnside stands the Free Church, a large barn-like building, ill suited to the needs of the congregation which assemble in it from week to week. It was an old "Cameronian" chapel, and, on good authority, it is said to be the oldest building in existence which was connected with that body. The congregation worshipped at first in the fields till, in 1783, a church of the most primitive character was erected. It was low in the ceiling, and thatched. Since then it has undergone some slight repairs. In 1849 three feet were added to the walls, and the old thatched roof gave place to the present slated roof. The present walls, with the exception of the slight addition and the brick passages, belong to the original fabric of last century. There is a flourishing and increasing congregation, to accommodate which the present building is found to be inadequate, and a new church is in contemplation. The present minister is John Somerville, B.D., settled in 1891.

In a central position in the village, also, there is a United Presbyterian Church, built in the year 1837. It is a neat square building, greatly enhanced by two low square towers, one at each of the front corners. The interior is light and comfortable. The present minister is William Rutherford, inducted 3d February, 1869.

Cockburnspath.

It was not till after the Reformation that Cockburnspath became a separate and independent parish. Previous to that it formed a chapelry of Oldhamstocks. It includes the ancient parish of Auldcambus, which belonged to the monastery of Coldingham as a cell of Durham.

Cockburnspath parish was made up of parts of Coldingham, Oldhamstocks, and Abbey St. Bathans. As a chapelry it is old, co-existent probably with the hospital, and both dating back to the thirteenth century.

The chapelry and hospital were in combination. The seal of Master Robert, the chaplain of Cockburnspath, is affixed to a charter given at Ayton in 1255. The title of Master belonged to the hospital—a leper hospital, no doubt—it was where some of the local victims of an incurable and loathsome disease found refuge and support.[*]

It is doubtful if the foundations of the present church, which are very old, are those of the ancient chapel. There is a place called Chapelhill, at some distance from Cockburnspath, near which there are indications of a graveyard having existed. This would probably be connected with the chapel.

---

[*] Dr. Hardy.—*Hist. Ber. Nat. Club.*

Whether the hospital with its chapel and burial-ground was located in the village is uncertain.*

In the Chartulary of the Priory of Coldingham is preserved a charter, by which William the Lion confirms a grant of half a carrucate of land to the hospital.†

The present church building is of a peculiar shape, its length being about 4½ times its breadth. The internal dimensions are 80 feet long and 18 feet 3 inches broad. At the west end of the church there is a curiously shaped tower or belfry. It is circular, and reaches to a height of 30 feet, its internal diameter being 6 feet, and the walls 15 inches thick. Its age is uncertain, but some anti-

---

* The chapelry and hospital are mentioned in the *Berwickshire Retours*, No. 145, Oct. 7, 1625, as being in possession of Master James Nicolsone de Cockbandspeth, and specified as "the Kirklands (still so named) of Auldhamstockis, lying in the Maynes, and within the vill of Cockbrandispeth, called 'Lie Hispitell.'"

† The following is a transcript of that charter, which has hitherto remained unpublished. Is is entitled "Confirmatio Donationis Hospitali de Aldcambus Facti":—"Willelmus Dei gratia Rex Scottorum omnibus probis hominibus totius terræ suæ clericis et laicis salutem. Sciant presentes et futuri me concessisse, et hac cartâ meâ confirmasse donationem illam, quam David de Quicheswde fecit Hospitali de Aldcambus et Leprosis ibi manentibus, de illa dimidia carucata terræ in Aldcambus quam Radulfus Pelliparius tenuit: tenendam in liberam et puram at perpetuam elemosinam, cum omnibus libertatibus et aisiamentis et predictam terram juste pertinentibus, ita liberé et quieté sicut carta predicti Davidis testatur: Salvo servicio meo. Testibus Willelmo de Bosch. Cancellario meo, Waltero Cuming. Davide de Hastings. Appud Jeddewrith, XVI. die Maij."—*Archæological Essays*, by the late Sir James Y. Simpson, Bart., M.D., D.C.L. In the foregoing Latin extract the original orthography is preserved.

quaries are inclined to regard it as very ancient. There are a number of apertures in its upper part which resemble the loopholes of peel towers, and suggest the idea of its having been erected as a watch tower.*

Near the east end of the building there are remains of a base course of early character; a buttress, with a rude pedimental head, is placed diagonally against each angle of the church; and the head of a window, of second-pointed date, has been preserved, and embedded in the south wall. This window has been of two foliated round-headed lights, with a quatre-foiled circle above, and over the whole is a pointed label terminating on each side in a kind of notch head.†

An old lintel has been inserted at this part, which is said to have been taken from another building having no connection with the church. It is inscribed thus:—

"I N   I H   1652."

When the more ancient part of the church was built no one has ever been able to discover. It is, however, an ancient structure; one of the stones taken from it, while undergoing repairs, bearing date 1163. It remained long in a most uncomfortable state, but repairs at various times have been made upon it, especially in 1807, when it was newly

---

* Macgibbon and Ross, who are perhaps the best authorities on such subjects, are of opinion that this tower dates back to the beginning of the sixteenth century. One feature, however, does seem to militate against this theory, and that is the thinness of its walls.

† Mr. Ferguson.—*Hist. Ber. Nat. Club*, 1890.

seated and rendered more comfortable, and again to a considerable extent in 1826.*

Surmounting the buttress at the south-west corner is a curious old sundial, which is supposed to date back to the beginning of the sixteenth century.†

The communion plate consists of two silver cups, engraved—" This cup belongs to the church of Cockburnspath. $_{II}^{M}s.$ M·1708."

The churchyard contains nothing specially interesting. The oldest stone now legible is a small one, inscribed thus :—

" Here . lyeth . John . Sinclar . who . departed . this . life 3th . of . May . 1726 . and . of his age . . .

On the other side of this stone are the death's head, cross bones, and hour glass.

---

* *New Statistical Account.*

† Referring to the sundials on the churches at Cockburnspath, Oldhamstocks, Macgibbon and Ross say :—" These are sloping dials, and, so far as our observation goes, they are unique amongst attached sundials, which are all upright ; and as these two dials probably date from early in the sixteenth century, they may be regarded as the forerunners of the ' lectern dials,' to be considered under a separate head. The dial at Cockburnspath forms the terminal of the angle buttress at the S.W. corner of the church ; its face leans forward, and the sides are splayed away ; the upper surface slopes backwards to the skew of the gable, and is hollowed like a half cylinder. A singular piece of stone sticks out like the stump of an amputated arm from the west side. Whether this was meant to tell the time by its shadow on the gable cannot be determined, as the wall is ' harled over.' The west end of this church, including the buttress and the singular round tower, as well as the east end, probably date from about the beginning of the sixteenth century, and without doubt the dial is part of the original structure."—Macgibbon and Ross' *Castellated and Domestic Architecture of Scotland from the Twelfth to the Eighteenth Century.*

The following beautiful lines appear on a nineteenth century stone :—

> " Dear is this spot where her dust sleeps,
> And sweet the strains her spirit pours ;
> Oh, why should we in anguish weep,
> She is not lost, but gone before."

There is an old handbell belonging to this parish, which is said to have been rung before funerals. It is encircled by three lines of inscriptions as follows :—

"Gifted . be . John . Henrie . Bower . in . Edinbvrgh . to . the . Sessione . and . Kirke . of . Cockburnspeth . 1650."

The church of Aldcambus, called St. Helen's Kirk, is situated three miles east from Cockburnspath, close to the sea shore. The writer of the Old Statistical Account, referring to its antiquity, says :—" From the nature of the building and other circumstances it is supposed to have been erected some time in the seventh century."

There is, unfortunately, no evidence to bear out this statement. A careful examination of the building by Mr. Muir in 1845 points to an origin not earlier than the first quarter of the twelfth century, although it may have replaced a structure of earlier date.

A considerable portion of the old building is still standing, but in quite a ruinous condition, surrounded by the old burial-ground. The ruin was pretty entire when examined by Mr. Muir in 1845, and the appearance of the place and its architectural features are described by him with great minuteness and accuracy :—

" This lonely and weather-beaten fragment of

early Christian art, with its little surrounding burial-ground, stands on an elevation overlooking the ocean, about three miles east of the village of Cockburnspath. It belongs to the Norman period, and consists of a chancel, internally 15 feet 6 inches long by 11 feet 5 inches wide; and nave, 30 feet 6 inches by 16 feet 11 inches.

" The nave is grievously reduced, but has still the remains of a south-east window and indications of a north-west doorway and vaulted roof. In the east end of the south wall, and close to the ground, is a plain square-edged, segmental-headed recess, 5 feet 9 inches wide and 9 inches deep; and immediately east of it is another of bisected form, with its crown abutting on the wall of the chancel-arch. The west wall, with its gable, is nearly perfect, though manifestly of later date. It has a plain triangular-headed buttress of three unequal stages placed diagonally on each corner; in all other respects, it is simply a mass of dead wall, in part, most likely, composed of wrecked portions of the ancient fabric, as the stones are nearly similar in size and shape to those in the building at large, and some of them, in the inner plane are hatched with the chevron moulding, and indubitably are parts of some of the windows or doorway arches.

" The separation of the chancel is very distinctly marked both internally and on the outside, but the whole compartment is very nearly in as ruinous a condition as the nave. Scarcely anything of the south wall is left, but the north and east elevations are tolerably entire: the former is blank; in the latter is a small, very slightly pointed light, a little recessed, under a shallow rectangular nook of the same form, 2 feet 4 inches long by 6 inches wide. It is quite plain, has its head of one stone, and opens upon the interior in a deep splay 5 feet high by 2 feet 11 inches wide. The inner aperture is semi-circular, and has a single hollow chevron carried round the head and down the sides close to the edges both outside and within.

"Of the chancel arch, which apparently has been of two chevroned orders, two or three of the voussoirs alone remain on each side; but the jambs are comparatively whole, and consist of four slender half-roll shafts, two grouped together under one double-escalloped capital, on each side of a large capitaled half-roll thrust prominently forward to meet the soffit-rib of the arch. None of the bases are visible. The capitals are quite perfect, very heavy, and had, as appears by a remnant, enormously ponderous abaci returned along the entire west face of the wall. The extant portion is on the north side. It is of the common trigonal form, and has its intermediate face, which is 7 inches broad, continued with a double row of continuously notched squares studded with saltiers, the rude typifications, doubtless, of the star-moulding of the more enriched example. Like that of mostly all the old churches of Scotland, the masonry is excellent. The material, however, does not seem of a very durable description. It is of that deep red colour common to many parts of the country, but which is more abundantly present in the buildings of this district, both ancient and modern. It is worthy of remark that the burial-ground north of the church does not appear ever to have been used for the purposes of interment."*

About a dozen stones are all that remain, and these are defaced and scattered about in a most shameful and dilapidated condition.

On a large horizontal stone are these words:—

"Here lyes Evphan Sebbald who departed this life the 6 of March 1672. Also Margret Atchison who departed this life the 27 of December 1697 and of hir age 41 years."

"Also James Suanston who departed this life the 15 of Agust 1717 and of his age 75 years."

Another large horizontal stone is inscribed thus:—

"Here lyes William Swanstown who departed this life the 9 of Febrwary 1711 and of his age 24 years."

The inscription on a large horizontal stone, with bevelled edges, is as follows:—

"Here lyes John Broun who departed this life the third of Jully 1686 and of his age 26 As also

"Here lyes William Roughead who departed this life the 26 of January 1710 and of his age 21 years."

An old horizontal stone, which was almost entirely covered over with turf, and lying considerably below the general level of the ground, has these words:—

"Heir lies John and Jenit Booklesses 1668 1669."

"Here lyes Georg Bookless who departed this life seuenth of Jun 1748."

Another horizontal stone bears the dates

"1646   1655,"

as well as initial letters, but, unfortunately, the latter are hidden by another large heavy stone.

---

* *Descriptive Notices of some of the Ancient Parochial and Collegiate Churches of Scotland*, by T. S. Muir, 1848.

This shows the utter confusion into which the place has been allowed to drift.

The following is a list of the ministers that have been in Cockburnspath since 1617:—

John Lauder (in Auldcambus)—1617 to 1627.
George Sydserfe, M.A.—1627 to 1639.
James Wright, M.A.—1640 to 1656.
Richard Callender, M.A.—1657 to 1663.
George Pollok, M.A.—1663 to 1671.
David Stirling, M.A.—1671 to 1681.
John Barclay, M.A.—1682 to 1689.
David Clunie, M.A.—1689 to 1700.
Henry Shaw—1702 to 1746.
David Spence—1748 to 1789.
Andrew Spence—1789 to 1844.
James Stirling (assistant and successor)—1805 to 1830.
Andrew Baird* (assistant and successor)—1831 to 1843.
William Paterson—1843 to 1863.
John M. Buchanan (assistant and successor)—1863 to 1869.
Joseph Hunter (assist. and suc., present incumbent)—1869.

There is a neat Free Church in the village of Cockburnspath, erected in 1890. The congregation formerly worshipped at Oldhamstocks. The present minister is David Hewitt, M.A., settled in 1882.

There is also a United Presbyterian Church at Stockbridge, in this parish. The present minister is Robert Simpson.

---

* Baird left the Established and joined the Free Church at the Disruption in 1843.—Scott's *Fasti*.

Coldingham.

In this parish there were two distinctly monastic institutions—that of St. Ebba's, founded in the seventh century, and that of Coldingham proper, founded in the eleventh century. Taking these in the order of time, as regards their origin, that of St. Ebba's falls to be dealt with first. Its great antiquity, and the romantic story of its origin, claim for St. Ebba's a very special and abiding interest. This monastery, which stood on the lofty promontory of St. Abb's Head, was founded in the year 670 by Princess Ebbe or Ebba, daughter of King Ethelfrid, and sister of Eanfrid, Oswald, and Oswin, successively kings of Bernicia. It seems that the pagan king of Mercia, or Mid-England, sought the hand of Princess Ebbe in marriage, and, to escape his solicitations, she left Northumberland, intending to seek refuge in East Anglia. On the voyage, however, her little bark was driven ashore by a storm, and she landed in a little creek on the coast of Berwickshire, at a place which is now known by her name. St. Abb's Head, a bold, dark-coloured headland, rises almost perpendicularly 306 feet above the waters of the German Ocean. Finding here a suitable spot, near where she had found a harbour of refuge from the storm, she resolved to found a convent in commemoration of the event, and in gratitude to God for her deliverance. Of this convent the princess became the first abbess.

The inmates of this religious house consisted of both monks and nuns; but the discipline was very rigid, and prevented all intercourse between the two sexes. Anxious to raise the monastery to a high moral standard, the abbess sent an urgent request to that holy man of God, St. Cuthbert, whose wonderful works in and around the monastery of Melrose had spread his fame abroad over all the land. Responding to this call, St. Cuthbert visited St. Abb's, and during a short sojourn in their midst he exercised a wonderful influence over the place and its inmates.

In the year 679 the monastery was consumed by fire, a calamity not so much the result of negligence as a judgment of heaven upon the inmates on account of their dissolute habits.

Again, in 870 it was plundered and destroyed by the Danes. On this occasion, it is said that the abbess, in order to preserve the chastity of the nuns, induced them to disfigure and mutilate their faces. This so enraged the barbarous invaders that they set fire to the buildings and massacred the inmates. This seems to have been the last of St. Ebba's convent, as there is no record of its having been rebuilt. Its career of two centuries, even from the little we know of it, was a somewhat checkered one.

The building, like all other ecclesiastical edifices of that period, would consist principally of timber, and a very rude affair it undoubtedly was. On the site of this convent are still to be traced the foundations of what appears to have been a chapel.

It is in the highest degree improbable that these could have formed the foundations of the original convent of St. Ebba's. They are more likely to be the remains of a chapel subordinate to the Priory of Coldingham, and erected many years after the demolition of St. Ebba's in 970.

Two miles south of St. Abb's is Coldingham Priory, an institution of much later date than St. Ebba's. It is perhaps as well here, in order to avoid confusion, to distinguish carefully between the monastery, as already noticed, founded in 670 on St. Abb's Head, and that which was founded about four centuries later at Coldingham. The monastery of St. Ebba's was practically extinct more than a century before that of Coldingham came into existence. The latter was not in any sense an offshoot or after-growth of the former.

The priory or monastery of Coldingham was founded in the year 1098 by Edgar, King of Scots, son of Malcolm Canmore, who, having been driven from his throne by a usurper, had fled to England, where he obtained from William Rufus an army of 30,000 men for the recovery of his dominions. Fordun tells us that on Edgar's march towards Scotland, St. Cuthbert appeared to him in a vision by night, promising him the protection of Heaven, and directing him to receive his consecrated banner from the convent of Durham, and to carry it before his troops, which if he did, his enemies would be dissipated and fly before him. Edgar related this dream to his uncle, Edgar Atheling, by whose advice he obeyed in all points the orders of the saint. The Abbot of Durham presented him with the banner, and he crossed the Tweed so confident in its virtues that it gave him the courage which insured success; and soon after he had succeeded in re-establishing his power he founded the monastery of Coldingham, which he dedicated to the Virgin Mary, and, in testimony of his gratitude to St. Cuthbert, he made a present of the place and lands belonging to it to the Benedictine monks of Durham.*

---

* William Brockie.—*A Brief Sketch of the History of the Priory of Coldingham.*

Several authorities, Mr. Brockie amongst them, maintain that a religious house existed here in very early times—many centuries prior to that which was founded by King Edgar in 1098. In support of this theory it would seem that, during the restoration of the priory in 1857, the workmen came upon the foundation walls of what is averred to have been the more ancient structure. Referring to those remains, another authority, Mr. King Hunter, in his admirable History of the Priory, says:—" The whole extent of these foundations was distinctly traceable; and this part of the building appears in the original, as in the after erection, to have formed the church of the monastery, but stretching a few feet further towards the south than the more recent structure. With the exception of the east end, it is of the same form—namely, an oblong square, of somewhat similar dimensions to the after priory. The east end consisted of a circular projection or apse—in all probability used as the chancel. The stone is of the same description as that of which the priory is built, of a reddish colour, and supposed to have been brought from a quarry called Greenheugh, in the parish of Cockburnspath, the nearest place where such stone is now to be found." Mr. Hunter goes on to prove at considerable length the existence of this early building, but his evidence, it seems to me, is, on the whole, insufficient to establish the fact. In the absence, therefore, of more reliable documentary evidence, I am inclined to think with Mr. Ferguson that the old foundations referred to are merely those of King Edgar's foundation.

This king, in his munificent liberality, endowed the priory with the whole village of Swinton, together with many other privileges. He granted to the priors the power of exercising ecclesiastical jurisdiction over the parishes of Eyemouth. Ayton, Lamberton, Auldcambus, Mordington, Chirnside, Buncle, and probably some others.

The office of prior in these days was not merely that of a purely ecclesiastical functionary. It is said that, while in the prime glory of his sacred and exalted station, he had a retinue of 70 functionaries— amongst these being the almoner, the master of the horse, the manager of the household, the receiver of guests, the keeper of the cellar, the brewer, &c.

Malcolm IV. (1153–1165) also extended his patronage to the priory, granting to the monks certain important privileges. William the Lion (1165–1214), in his turn, invested the prior with power to exact a heavy penalty from all who were found hunting in the woods or on the moors of Coldinghamshire without his permission; and to enforce these conditions he had a forester with ample salary settled amongst them.

About the church of Coldingham we are not so well informed. It is supposed to have been founded soon after the institution of the priory, although we have no documentary evidence to that effect amongst the Coldingham records. The first notice of it that we find in the chartulary is in a deed granted upwards of a hundred years later. We know, however, that in 1127 Robert, Bishop of St. Andrews, granted to the church of Coldingham freedom and exemption from all episcopal aids, such as Custom, Can, or Cuneved (in Gaelic, Canmhath), meaning "first fruits." The church was a cell or dependency attached to the monastery, and its advowson was vested in the prior and chapter of the monks.*

In the years 1292 and 1296 Henry de Horncastre, then prior of Coldingham, with the other clergy of Coldinghamshire, swore fealty to Edward I. at Berwick, and were accordingly reinvested in their offices.

Coldingham, during the fierce wars between England and Scotland, shared in the general misfortunes and vicissitudes common to all the religious institutions in the south of Scotland, more so, indeed, from the fact of its being a dependency of Durham, thus laying it open to attacks from English and Scots alike.

During the turbulent regency of the Duke of Albany, in the beginning of the fifteenth century, the priory came under the protection of the powerful Archibald, Earl of Douglas, one of whose dependents, the Laird of Home, in the Merse, became its sub-prior.

A few years later William Douglas, Earl of Angus and Lord of Liddesdale, became special protector and defender of the priory and its appurtenances, for which he received a liberal salary.

In 1528, during an incursion by the English, the abbey was partly consumed by fire.

In 1488 an attempt was made on the part of King James III. to suppress the priory, but a

---

* Mr. Brockie.—*History of Coldingham Priory.*

number of powerful barons—amongst them the Homes, the Hepburns, and the Earl of Angus—joined in a conspiracy against the King, which resulted in his defeat and death at Stirling.

By Act of Parliament, in 1504, the priory was annexed to the Crown, and in 1509 it ceased to have any connection with Durham, and became annexed to the abbey of Dunfermline, under whose jurisdiction it continued till 1560, a year which witnessed the overthrow of all the monasteries of Scotland.

In 1544 the English made an incursion into the Merse, and marched towards Coldingham. They seized the abbey, and fortified the church and church tower. In the following year the noble abbey, which had stood for nearly 500 years, was burned down by that inveterate despoiler, the Earl of Hertford. A century later appeared that moral scourge, Oliver Cromwell, who blasted everything having the smallest semblance of Popery, and disfigured some of the finest monuments of architectural beauty, such as no chisel or art has since been able to surpass.

In 1648 Cromwell completed the ruin of the church, which had been fortified by the Royalists, by blowing it up with gunpowder after the capitulation of the garrison. Only the east and north walls of the choir, with a tower, affirmed by Carr to have stood at the north-west angle of the transept, but which was probably the central tower, or a reconstruction of it, and some portions of the transepts themselves and of the monastic buildings were left standing. A south and a west wall were subsequently added to the choir to convert it into a parish church; and it is to this fortunate circumstance that we owe the preservation of the scanty remains of the once glorious fabric. The tower already mentioned fell about a century ago, and its ruins, as well as those of the other portions of the priory not used for divine service, became the prey of every heritor and householder in the neighbourhood who was in need of materials for building.*

Since the beginning of this century, however, a better spirit has set in, so that what the barbarians had left of these sacred edifices, is now carefully preserved. The choir of Coldingham Abbey Church, which had been used as the parish church for nearly three hundred years, was put in good order by the heritors in 1857. The first step in the restoration was to strip the church of its cumbrous internal fittings—galleries, pews, &c.—and restore the building to the state in which it was left in the days of Cromwell, but further mutilated and defaced by the rude hand of time, and the more rude and destructive hand of man. The next was to remove a large depth of earth from the internal area, lowering the floor about six feet, and exhibiting a corresponding portion of the decorated wall hitherto lost to view. On the outside the earth was excavated to the base of the building. Thus the ruin stood naked to view, presenting the north and east walls of the ancient building. The west wall was next rebuilt in the original style, and also the south wall in a style approaching to the ancient,

---

* Mr. Ferguson.—*Hist. Ber. Nat. Club*, 1890.

but, on account of the expense, without its old decorations. The corner towers were carried up as they were supposed to have existed originally. The roof was to a considerable extent renewed, the ceiling having been replaced with polished stained wood, in imitation of oak. The whole of the beautiful architectural decorations were cleared of the unseemly coatings of white; and those parts which were effaced and mutilated were thoroughly restored, and all broken pillars and bases, where incapable of repair, were replaced by new ones of so close an imitation as scarcely to be distinguishable. The general cathedral-like effect is grand and imposing, there being no galleries, and the character and arrangement of the pews and fittings being in strict conformity with the building.*

The architectural features of the north and east walls of the choir—by far the oldest portion of the building, not the remains of King Edgar's foundation, however, but of a restoration in the end of the twelfth or beginning of the thirteenth century—are thus faithfully and minutely described by Mr. Muir:—

"The style of the architecture is partly Norman and partly First Pointed; neither, however, quite pure, but each slightly dashed, as it were, with a tinge of the other. Externally, the north elevation exhibits some single light lancet windows, divided from one another by broad shallow buttresses projecting only a few inches from the wall. The head mouldings of the windows are composed of half and

---

* Mr. Brockie.—*History of Coldingham Priory.*

three-quarter rounds deeply under-cut, rising from banded edge-shafts, with floriated capitals and annular bases, resting on a circle of balls.

"Besides the Norman character of the buttresses, additional indications of a style earlier than that shown in the general form and details of the windows may be traced in the square-shaped abaci of the shafts, and in the foliage of the capitals, which has much of the thin, wiry, and rather meagre execution of the floriations belonging to the Transition or Semi-Norman period.

"The same modification, or rather admixture of styles, is also observable in the Norman arcade, which occupies the under compartment of the elevation. This ornamental feature is arranged in couplets below the windows, and separated from them by a narrow trigonal string, which, after coursing their cills and making a slight vertical descent a little beyond the line of the jambs, terminates in a horizontal return across the buttresses, dividing them about midway. The semi-circular arches fill the whole breadth of each compartment, and are composed of a small sharp-edged triangular moulding set between quarter and half-rounds, with a bold trigonal drip over. These spring from single cylindrical edge-shafts, with Norman abaci and First Pointed capitals, and two central bearing shafts of the same form, engaged by a small semi-octagonal member sunk between.

"Regarding the east end of the building little requires to be said. In arrangement, style, and detail, it agrees very closely with the portion already described. The wall is nearly entire, and is flanked by square turrets, with cylindrical shafts sunk in their angles. The bases of the turrets are moulded, and their heads have sloping roofs, after the manner of set-offs, which give to these adjuncts much of the appearance of ponderous buttresses. In the north one each of the two stages, formed by the string course, is pierced with a narrow lancet-headed slit. The facade between the turrets contains three windows similar to those in the north wall, divided also by wide pilasters. The arcade below is likewise in conformity in all respects, excepting as regards the mouldings, which are chevroned.

"The same order in the disposition of parts observed in the outside is maintained in the interior; but, besides greater coherence of style, there is a singularity in the constructional form which has a peculiarly rich and striking effect. An open arcade, formed in the thickness of the wall, and in appearance resembling a triforium, is carried along the upper compartment, of sufficient depth to admit of free passage round the building. The arches are set in couplets between the windows, by which they are divided apart, but without disturbing the continuity, as their heads are so contrived as to combine with, and to give a beautiful variety of form to, the general arrangement. The faces of the arches are finely moulded with a series of rounds, individually relieved by deep undercuttings. The bearing shafts are of two kinds—those nearest the windows are semi-cylindrical triple clusters, the outer or projecting member being a little pointed;

the intermediate ones are composed of two half-rounds, with a semi-octagonal moulding between. The bases belonging to both kinds are rolls maintaining the plan of the shaft, and are set on square plinths, the outer faces of which are flush with the plane of the subjacent wall. Single cylindrical shafts, resting on the abaci of the shafts below, are also attached to the edges of the window-jambs, and from them the mouldings of the archivolt have their spring.

"In the shape of the arches, grouping of the mouldings, and configuration of the most of the minor details, there is here to be observed a much nearer approach to integrity of style than is to be found on the external edifice. The capitals, however, still retain the square abacus; and the foliage, although better developed and more varied in design than is usually to be met with among early Semi-Norman structures, is yet awanting in the prominence, and that peculiar freedom and sweetness of turn so conspicuous in the herbaceous forms of the mature First-Pointed period."*

About a mile to the east of St. Ebba's monastery is the site of another chapel and burying-ground. Half-a-century ago the remains of this chapel were considerable. Now a series of grassy mounds, with fragments of masonry appearing here and there above the surface, are all that remain.

Near Reston, in this parish, there existed a chapel

---

* *Descriptive Notices of some of the Parochial and Collegiate Churches of Scotland*, by T. S. Muir.

dedicated to St. Nicholas. It is styled in one of the Coldingham charters, " The chapel of St. Nicholas, situated in the vill of West Riston." Its exact site, however, is not known.

The priory of Coldingham possessed the privilege of sanctuary; and a number of crosses were erected in various parts of the neighbourhood, probably to mark the strict boundaries of the asylum. In a wooded hollow called The Dean, near the village, is a spring known as " St. Andrew's Well," which formerly supplied the priory with water, and is still in use.*

In 1446 the priory contained 2 cups (one gilt, the other silvered), a thurible, a cup of tin, and a pair of cruets.

It seems that Mr. Alexander Douglas (1677–1689), the previous Episcopalian incumbent, who had retired with a considerable number of parishioners to worship in a barn near the church, carried off, along with other things, the communion plate. Mr. John Dysart, who was inducted minister of the parish in place of Mr. Douglas, caused a deputation to go to the latter and demand the pulpit Bible, communion cups, baptismal basin, the boxes for collection, and the box for the communion cloth and mortcloth, which he had carried off. It appears from the Kirk Session Records that most of these articles belonging to the church were retained by Mr. Douglas, who resisted all appeals.

There are two silver cups, engraved—" The money for buying this was left as a legacy by John

---

* Mr. Ferguson.—*Hist. Ber. Nat. Club*, 1890.

Smith of Smithfield, and payed by John Edington, his executor and successor, on fifteenth of February, 1728."

The following is a list of the churches and chapels held by the priory in the county:—

The chapels of St. Ebba (on St. Abb's Head), Eyemouth, Ayton, and St. Nicholas, West Reston. The churches of Lamberton, Fishwick, Swinton, Edrom (with its chapels of Kimmerghame, East Nisbet, Blackadder, and Earlston). Aldcambus, with its hospital. Also the chapels of Naithansthirn and Newton, subordinate to Ednam. These were subsequently acquired by Kelso Abbey.*

Several floor-crosses and other sepulchral slabs have been collected, and placed against the exterior of the south transept wall. On one of these a portion only of the inscription is decipherable, and reads thus:—

"HEIR WIS BVRIED
JAMES AND MARGART
CHISOMME 1562."

In the churchyard, which is large, there is nothing very remarkable.

On a very small stone are these words:—

"Here lyes the corps of Jean Bookless who departed this life the 19 Awgwst 1741 aged 67 st years."

The following pathetic and simple words appear on the bottom of a modern stone erected to the memory of a young wife:—

"I will follow the wife of my youth."

* Mr. Ferguson.—*Hist. Ber. Nat. Club*, 1890.

On a very small stone is this inscription:—

" Here. lyes. the. corps. of. James. Alensha. who. deperted this. life. September. 24. 1727."

The following initials and dates appear on a very small stone:—

" I.   P.
   1661.
  I.   H.
   1670."

During the reparations already referred to, the tombs of two of the priors—Ærnaldus and Radulphus—who presided over the establishment about the beginning of the thirteenth century, were found within a square apartment, near the west end of the building. The two large slabs are now carefully protected by means of a strong iron grating over the top, and are thus inscribed:—

" Ærnaldus prior 1202."

" Radvlphvs prior de Coldingham 1209."

These lines appear on a modern tombstone:—

" All ye who read my epitaph,
Seek ye the Lord and put not off;
Remember, when my grave you see,
I once did live like unto thee;
But soon by death was snatched away
In bloom of youth and no decay;
Oh! for eternity prepare,
And make a future life thy care."

The following is a list of the ministers that have been in Coldingham since 1567:—

William Lamb—1567 to 1583.
David Hume—1585 to 1592.
Alexander Watsone, M.A.—1593 to 1614.
William Douglas—1615 to 1621.

Christopher Knoues, M.A.—1622 to 1641.
Samuel Douglas, M.A.—1641 to 1652.
David Hume, M.A.—1658 to 1662.*
Alexander Hewat, M.A.—1665 to 1665 (a few months).
Andrew Bannatin, M.A.—1665 to 1668.
Alexander Douglas, M.A.—1677 to 1689.
John Dysart, M.A.—1694 to 1732.†
Robert Brydone, M.A. (colleague and successor)—1725 to 1761.
John Jolly—1761 to 1792.
James Landell—1793 to 1827.
James Home Robertson—1827 to 1847.
David Munro (present incumbent)—1847.

A chapel-of-ease was erected at Renton by the Presbytery, 14th and opened 26th January, 1794. The following were ministers:—

Joseph Bethune—1794 to 1799.
George Marshall—1800 to 1811.

At HOUNDWOOD there is a church which was built and opened in 1836, constituted as a *quoad sacra* parish by the General Assembly, 30th May, 1836, and 28th May, 1838, and erected as such by the

---

* This David Hume joined the field preachers in 1679; he was present at the battle of Bothwell Brig same year, and, being obliged to flee, took refuge in Holland, and was one of the numerous body declared fugitive 5th May, 1684. He returned, however, and died in Edinburgh, 13th Dec., 1687, aged about 62; and has been represented as "of known zeal, piety, courage, and ability."—Scott's *Fasti Ecclesiæ Scoticanæ.*

† Dysart was a man of bold and determined character, ever ready to defend the Presbyterian cause, and zealous in maintaining what he considered the interests of the Church. The great body of the parishioners being of the Episcopal persuasion, it was found necessary to call a military force to prevent a riot at the settlement, and such was his dread of opposition that, for a time, he was obliged to carry pistols with him to the pulpit, which he laid down openly on each side of him.—Scott's *Fasti Ecclesiæ Scoticanæ.*

Court of Teinds, 9th July, 1851. The building is a plain quadrangular structure of red stone, with a square belfry tower engaged in the front elevation, and terminating in a low pyramidal slated roof. It came in place of the old chapel-of-ease at Renton already referred to.

The list of ministers is as follows:—

> John Duncan—1836 to 1837.
> John Robertson—1838 to 1843.
> David Drummond—1851 to 1879.
> George A. Bisset (present incumbent)—1880.

There is a United Presbyterian Church in the village of Coldingham. It was originally built in 1793, and was rebuilt in 1870. The present minister is Andrew Brodie Robertson, settled in 1856.

At St. Abb's, in this parish, there is a Free Church—a neat edifice of simple Norman style; quite a model little church; erected in 1892. The present minister is John S. Allison, settled in 1895.

At Grant's-House, also in this parish, there is a Free Church, erected in 1888. (Formerly the congregation worshipped at Houndwood.) The building is neat, commodious, and, inside, exceedingly comfortable. The present minister is James Marshall, M.A., B.D., settled (first at Houndwood) in 1882.

There is also a Free Church at Reston, erected in 1880. It is in the Early English style, neat and ornamental. The present minister is William Hall Telford, settled in 1881.

Coldstream.

In this parish in early times a Cistercian convent or priory stood near the junction of the Leet with the Tweed. It was founded and dedicated to the Virgin Mary by Cospatrick, 3d Earl of Dunbar, in the year 1165. In his foundation charter, Earl Cospatrick associated himself with Derder, his countess, and personally bestowed on the nuns a' carucate—that is, from sixty to a hundred acres—of the Hirsel, and the church of that place. The Hirsel, which is situated about a mile to the north-west of Coldstream, forms the beautiful seat of the Earl of Home.

The following is an abstract of charter granted about the year 1232, which shows the relation of Hirsel church to Coldstream Priory:—" To all the sons of Holy Mother Church, William, the son of Patrick, greeting. At the bidding of charity has given and granted to God, and the Church of St. Mary of Caldstrem, and the nuns there serving God, the Church Herissille, with its lands, tithes, and offerings, and all other just pertinents of said church, in free, pure, and perpetual alms, as freely and quietly as the charters of Earl Cospatrick, and Earl Waldeve, and Patrick, the granter's father, witness and confirm, and as any church in the kingdom of Scotland is more freely, quietly, honourably, and fully held."

Another church belonging to the Priory was that of Lennel (the name of the parish prior to 1716). From another old charter, granted near the beginning of the 13th century, we learn that "Earl Patrick of Dunbar confirms to God and the holy nuns of Caldestrem, the whole church of Laynall with all its pertinents, to be held in perpetual alms, as the charters of his predecessors Earl Cospatrick and Earl Waldeve, his father, attest." (The Earl Patrick here referred to died in 1232.)

During the Border wars this convent suffered severely. Edward I. on his way northward encamped at Coldstream with 5000 horse and 30,000 infantry. On this occasion the priory and its orchard suffered great damage, for which, however, compensation was demanded and granted.

In the year 1472, on 6th June, James III. confirmed the charter under the great seal granted at Perth on 23d July, 1459, whereby his royal predecessor, James II., bestowed on the convent of Coldstream the lands of Simpryn (Simprim).

In 1515—two years after the battle of Flodden— Lord Dacre thus wrote to Margaret the Queen mother of Scotland, who had besought his protection in behalf of the prioress (Isabella of Coldstream) and sisters:—"Madam, In my mooste humble wise I recommended me unto your grace. And where it hath pleased you too desire me for your sake too cause all Englishmen too forbere to doo any hurtis unto the priores of Coldstreme and hir hous, madame, I shall with good will obserue your commaundemente and pleasure, she and hers doing ner supporting any too doo hurte to the king, my sourain lord's subiects, ner keeping ner receiving into hir hous any Scottishemen of war."

The last ruler of the convent was Dame Janet Hoppringill, during whose tenure of office the structure was burned to the ground by the Earl of Hertford in 1545.*

Not a vestige of the convent buildings is now remaining. The pomarium of the priory is now represented by a large orchard occupying a considerable space at the south-west side of the town sloping down towards the site of the buildings.† Tradition states that many of the Scottish nobles who fell at Flodden were brought to Coldstream and interred in the priory burial-ground. In 1834, during excavations at the place, many human bones and a stone coffin were exposed to view.

There is a tradition to the effect that the bell of the convent was carried by the English to Durham, and suspended in the cathedral of that city.

---

* The election of Dame Janet Hoppringill as prioress was an interesting and important ceremony: the nuns having assembled for the purpose "directed their wishes, with one voice and one breath, upon Dame Janet Hoppringill, a veiled and professed sister of their house, marked out by her virtues as the person most fit, worthy, and qualified, circumspect in spirituals and temporals, and for the rule and governance of their said monastery and its revenues, most able, expert, and industrious, arrived at lawful age, born of lawful matrimony and of honourable parents, above others expert in the rule and religion of the monastery, and elected the said Dame Janet as their prioress and pastress of their souls."—Extract from the Instrument of Election of Dame Janet Hoppringill as prioress of Coldstream.

† In 1621 it was spoken of as the "litle croft, callit the lyttle orchard," and in 1640 it was styled the "little croft called the pomarium."

The church or chapel of Hirsel had disappeared as early as 1627, though the churchyard was then in use.

The church of Bassendean also belonged to the monastery of Coldstream. It is noticed at considerable length under WESTRUTHER, to which parish it now belongs.

The ancient church of LENNEL stood on the north bank of the Tweed, rather more than a mile to the north-east of Coldstream. The west gable, portions of the north and south walls of the nave, and indications of a narrower chancel are still extant. The nave has been 54 feet long by 22½ feet wide externally, but the dimensions of the chancel cannot be satisfactorily determined. On the south side of the nave are traces of a doorway, with a segmental head and slightly moulded jambs, and of two hollow-chamfered windows, which have opened to the interior with a wide lateral splay, and a segmental rear-arch. The west elevation has evidently undergone alterations at a late period. It is crow-stepped, and is pierced by two rectangular windows, both plainly bevelled on the outside; the upper, 3½ feet by 22 inches; the lower, which is blocked, 26 inches by 18 inches. Such details as are still visible are meagre in the extreme, but some of them can hardly be later than the close of the 12th century.*

An old hand-bell which had been rung for funerals and other purposes, and which was afterwards used

---

* Mr Ferguson.—*Hist. Ber. Nat. Club*, 1890.

in Coldstream, is still in existence, and bears the following inscription :—

"This is Lendon Hand Bel."

The following extract from an official Report shows the state of ecclesiastical affairs in this parish in the year 1627 :—

"The said parish conteins thrie myllis in length and two myllis in breadth the eistmost toune of the parish is distant from the said kirk ane myll and half myll the westmost ane myll and half myll the northmost toune two mylles. Ther is no toune of the said parish on the south the kirk standing vpon the river of Tueid.

"As for any vnion of the said kirk to any other, or of any other kirk to it we know none.

"The kirk of Lendell is ane kirk of the Pryorie of Cauldstreame it was of old bot ane chappell callit Lendell chappell and now it is the parish kirk be reasone of the most commodious situation for the parish. As for cheplanries we know none to be within our said parish bot ther hes bein of old neir to the Hirsell ather chappell or kirk quhair of ther is onlie restand ane kirk yaird callit Granton kirkyard possessit be the Earle of Home and we know no benefeit belonging thairto.

"Written out and signed at Lenddell kirk the tuentie day of Maij the yeir of God $I^{m.}$ $VI^{c.}$ tuentie sevin yeiris."

The present church of this parish stands about the centre of the town of Coldstream. It was erected in 1716, renovated and repaired in 1798.

It is commodious and comfortable, but, exterior and interior alike, severely plain.

Surrounding the ruined church at Lennel is the old churchyard, which contains some interesting stones.

On a medium-sized stone the latter part of the inscription only is decipherable, and runs thus:—

"To Lavrance Bell in Nevcastell vho departed this lyfe the 9 of 1689 December."

A very small peculiarly shaped stone bears along its upper curved surface, in letters almost completely obliterated, the following:—

"Heir lyes . . . Wleken (?) who dep . . 1655."

On the sides of this stone are engraved the death's head, hour glass, and cross bones.

Another similarly shaped stone is thus inscribed:—

"Heir . lyes . Robrt . Paterson . vho . dp . the . 15 . April 1664."

On a small, plain stone are the words:—

"Here lyeth the body of John Kers who deceased the 6 day of October 1694 his age 32 years."

A large horizontal stone is inscribed in large striking characters:—

"I.   F.
    1658.
   B.   B."

These words appear on a small stone:—

"Here lyes the body of John don vho departed this life vpon the 2 day of nover 1699.. His age 56 years."

A medium-sized stone, which is sadly mutilated and defaced, the upper part being broken off, is inscribed thus :—

"James Wa .. sone to Alixander Watsone dyir in Calstream he died the 4 of July 1686.
"Jean Watsone died 28 of May 1683."

The inscription on a large horizontal stone runs thus:—

"Here on the sowth side of this stone at a small distance lyes the body of John Bell of Rwtchester rig who dy'd Jwne 1st A.D. 1729 aged 55 years. On his left hand lyes Margt. Donaldson his spowse who dy'd Janwary 4th A.D. 1743 aged 77 years. On his right hand lyes the body of Elizabeth Wrie relect of Charles Bell of Craigfoody who dy'd Septr. 11th A.D. 1742 aged 62 years. Wnder this stone lyes the body of George Bell of Rwtchester Rige who dy'd October 4th A.D. 1742 aged 36 years."

On the bottom of this stone are the words:—

"His father and his mother dear his brothers and his sisters were buried here."*

An elegant stone is erected to the memory of the Rev. Adam Thomson, D.D., minister of the United Presbyterian Church, Coldstream; died 23d February, 1861. His many excellent qualities are

---

* I am indebted to the Rev. Robert Paul, Dollar (formerly of Coldstream), for the following note, as well as for copies of several of the inscriptions in Lennel churchyard as given in the text, and copied by him at a time when they were more easily deciphered :—

"In 1801, John Bell and Betty Bell of Berwick—the representatives of the family thus commemorated—gave a donation of £500 to the minister and kirk-session of Coldstream for the education of the poor of the parish, to which they added £300 in 1803 for clothing for the children of the poor on leaving school."

set forth in a lengthy inscription, which concludes thus:—

"The great success of his career was the abolition of the Scottish Bible monopoly, along with what he did and suffered for the cheapening and circulation of the holy book."

A son thus comments on his mother:—

"I owe thee much : thou hast deserved from me
Far, far beyond what I can ever pay ;
Oft have I proved the labours of thy love
And the warm efforts of thy gentle heart."

By these touching lines David Innes celebrates his wife:—

"Clos'd, ever clos'd those speaking eyes,
　Where sweetness beam'd, where candour shone ;
And silent that heart-thrilling voice,
　Which music lov'd and call'd her own.
Alas ! before the violet bloom'd,
　Before the snows of winter fled,
Too certain fate my hopes consum'd,
　For she was numbered with the dead."

William Beloe laments his wife thus:—

"Oft to this spot
　Will memory fondly turn,
And love's pure flame
　Still unextinguished burn
Within their breasts, who
　Here doth mourn their loss,
But nails their sorrows
　To a Saviour's cross.
Oh ! precious hope !
　By faith to mortals given,
That loving hearts which
　Hath on earth been riven,
May through the same
　Dear Saviour's pleading love
Again unite in realms
　Of bliss above."

On an upright stone in the south-east portion of the churchyard :—

"To the memory of John Hume, Tenant in Easter Bankhead of Eccles, who was born at Easter Coldstream on 7th June, 1716, and interred here in 1785; and to several of his immediate ancestors also interred here, who suffered severely during the period between 1638 and 1689 in the noble effort to preserve unimpaired the civil and religious liberties of Scotland against Prelatic oppression; one having fallen in a field of conflict in this neighbourhood, while others experienced persecution and confiscation of property. Erected by his grandson, John Hume of the Register House, Edinburgh, 1837."

On a mural tablet, on the inner (eastern) side of the western gable of the old church, in the lower part of the watch-house, now used as the sexton's tool-house :—

"Here lies the body of Robert Blackie, late surgeon in Coldstream, who died July 4th, 1780, aged 36 years.

"No private interest did his soul invade,
No foe he injured, no kind friend betrayed;
He followed virtue as his truest guide,
Lived like a Christian, like a Christian died.

This monument was erected by his widow, Margaret Denholm, in remembrance of him."

On a stone, much sunk in the ground, in the south-east part of the churchyard, is this inscription :—

"This ston is erected by Vilam Shirif . in . remmemberance . of . his . davter . Margret . Shirif . vho . departed . this . lyf . in . the . year . of . God . 1698."

The following is a list of the ministers that have been in Coldstream since 1576 :—

John Clapperton—1576 to 1617.
Francis Hepburne, M.A.—1617 to 1632.
Thomas Hepburn, M.A.—1641 to 1642.
James Home—1642 to 1653.
Wm. Johnstone, M.A.—1659 to 1662.
David Robertson, M.A.—1663 to 1685.
Thomas Blair, M.A.—1686 to 1689.
James Armstrang—1690 to 1694.
John Pow, M.A.—1694 to 1735.
William Wilsone, M.A.—1735 to 1777.
James Bell—1778 to 1794.
Robert Scott—1795 to 1830.
Thomas Smith Goldie—1830 to 1859.
Archibald Nisbett (present incumbent)—1860.

There is a handsome Free Church here, erected in 1847, enlarged and improved in 1891. Its square tower, 80 feet high, is one of the conspicuous features of the town, being visible on all sides from a great distance. The present minister is James Rutherford, B.D., settled in 1887.

The East United Presbyterian Church was erected in 1826. It is a large building—of the old tea-caddy shape—and seated for 800. The present minister is John Lockhart Elder, M.A., settled in 1882.

The West United Presbyterian Church was built in 1806. It is a large square building, exceedingly plain and unpretentious. Recent alterations have greatly improved the interior in appearance and comfort. The present minister is Archibald Macaulay Caldwell, settled in 1892.

Cranshaws.

WE have no information as to the origin of the church of Cranshaws. Mention is made of it in the year 1296, but undoubtedly it existed a considerable time before that. Robert de Strivelin, the parson of the church of Cranshaws, swore fealty to Edward I. in 1296, and, in consequence, had his rights restored. The church contained an altar to St. Ninian, to whom also, in all probability, it was dedicated.

Alexander Swinton, member of a noted Border family, was minister of Cranshaws from 1592 to 1595. In his time an incident occurred, the memory of which is said to be preserved by a mural tablet in Cranshaws Parish Church. It is said that one of the Stewart kings—at the date referred to it must have been James VI.—being on a visit at Yester, rode across the hills to Cranshaws, and attended service in the church, when the minister, disconcerted, it may have been, by the royal presence, omitted the usual prayer for His Majesty. The story goes on to say that, in order to keep him and his successors in all time coming mindful of their duty in this respect, the King caused the tablet referred to, bearing the royal arms, to be placed opposite the pulpit. There it remained, till removed to a similar position in the existing church, when the old one was taken down.*

Only a small fragment of the old church remains in the shape of the foundations and part of the east wall. The church has been of a lengthy, oblong shape, with a vestry at the west end. There were two doors to the south with flagged entries. A portion of the roughly-built remains (left by the heritors to show the substantiality of the original walls when compelled to erect a new kirk), which had beneath it a still older wall. The floor was cleared out, and a large number of crania placed together were come upon underneath. Two crania of extraordinary proportions were connected with some gigantic thigh bones. Five oyster shells were turned out, some coffin handles, and some slips of zinc or lead for enclosing window glass.†

The old burial-ground, now in disuse, surrounding the old church, is in a most sadly dilapidated condition—tombstones lying about in the utmost confusion and disorder.

On a very small, thick stone are these words along the top:—

"Alexander Foord 1665."

On the face of the stone on one side are rather neatly carved an hour glass and hand bell, the latter probably emblematical of the office of sexton.

Another small stone is inscribed thus:—

"Here lyes John Dodd who departed this life Decembr 9 1717."

---

* *The Swintons of that Ilk.*
† Dr. Hardy.—*Hist. Ber. Nat. Club.*

On a similar stone are the words :—

"Here lyeth John Hog died Nov. 1681 & John Hog he died in Avgvst 1680 & Thomas Hog 1686."

A small stone, much broken and lying flat on the ground, has these words inscribed on a small oval panel :—

"Here lyes the corps of Janet Fortune who died Jan y^o 8 1728 age 12 years."

A large, handsome stone, whose inscription is quite illegible, bears some beautiful and highly ornamental carvings—the death's head, cross bones, hour glass, and spade.

The present church is situated a considerable distance from the ancient building. It was erected in 1739. Half-a-century ago it was described as probably in a worse state of repair than any Established Church in the south of Scotland. In fact, both church and manse were in a much worse state than most hunting stables in the county.*

In the north interior wall of the church is inserted a mural tablet, on which are sculptured the arms of the Royal House of Stuart, the interesting tradition concerning which has already been given. The church, both exterior and interior, is exceedingly plain.

In the modern churchyard there is nothing of interest; the stones, about a dozen in all, being comparatively modern.

---

* *New Statistical Account.*

The following is a list of the ministers of Cranshaws since 1572 :—

Matthew Liddell—1572 to 1585.
Alexander Swyntoun, M.A.—1593 to 1595.
John Hepburne, M.A.—1596 to 1611.
Mungo Daliell, M.A.—1615 to 1652.
John Foord—1655 to 1674.
John Suinton, M.A.—1674 to 1706.
John Campbel, M.A.—1706 to 1759.
Richard Scot--1759 to 1761.
Ralph Drummond - 1762 to 1784.
George Drummond—1785 to 1792.
Alexander Johnston—1792 to 1800.
David Tod, M.A.—1801 to 1813.
James Hope Sibbald—1813 to 1853.
William Menzies Hutton, M.A.—1853 to 1876.
James Forbes—1876 to 1879.
R. Bridges Smith (present incumbent)—1879.

Duns.

No existing records give us any information as to when the original church of Duns was erected. That a church did exist here in early times—probably about the middle of the twelfth century—is certain; beyond this we know nothing.

Mention is made of the church in the year 1296 when Henry de Lematon, rector of Duns, took the oath of allegiance to Edward I. at Berwick.

In the reign of David II. (1329–1370), Patrick, Earl of Dunbar, when he founded the collegiate church of Dunbar, annexed to it the church of Duns as one of its prebends.*

It is probable that the old church was repaired in the year 1572, as that date was carved in front of the burgess loft in the old building. Not a vestige, however, of this original structure remains, the last of it having been removed in 1874.

After the Reformation the chancel seems to have been converted into a burial-aisle by the Wedderburn family, the north and south transepts being simultaneously appropriated for the same purpose by the proprietors of Duns Castle and Manderston respectively. The two transepts, with the nave, which had been repaired and fitted up for Presby-

---

* Chalmers' *Caledonia*.

terian worship, were wholly demolished in the operations of 1790; but the Wedderburn aisle remained until 1874, when, as already stated, it was removed, at the instigation of the minister of the parish, in the course of some improvements which were being carried out on the churchyard. A stone coffin, found in excavating a grave within the church in 1736, was removed in 1790 to the manse, where it was utilised for many years as a watering trough, and finally destroyed by the minister about 1830. Such was the manner in which the antiquities of the parish were dealt with by those who might have been expected to take the chief interest in their preservation.*

Near the farm steading of Chapel, and a little to the south of it, about three miles north-west of Duns, stood at one time a chapel, which was dedicated to St. Mary Magdalene.† The last vestige of this structure was dug up and removed in 1808. The building was rectangular in form, and exceedingly plain, possessing no features of architectural interest. A graveyard surrounded the chapel, and a number of old tombstones lay scattered about at the period above mentioned, but these have also entirely disappeared.

In the Papal Taxation Roll of Churches and Monasteries in Scotland, drawn up in the early part of the reign of Edward I., mention is made of a hospital called "Bona Hospitalis de Duns," the value of which is returned at LXVIII^s. Nothing is known

---

* Mr. Ferguson.—*Hist. Ber. Nat. Club,* 1890.
† *Retours, Berwickshire.*

of either its site or history. The chapel above described may have been connected with it; but this is a pure conjecture, deriving, however, some probability from the fact that St. Mary Magdalene, to whom the chapel was dedicated, was the patron saint of numerous hospitals throughout the country.*

In the churchyard, on the site of the chancel of the old church, is the private burial-ground of the Homes of Wedderburn. The first of that family was buried here in 1470. In the year 1608 an aisle was erected upon it; on the lintel of its front entrance is the inscription :—

"Death cannot sinder   S. G. H.   D. I. H.   1608.

(These initials signify—Sir George Home. Dame Isabell Home.)

"Home of Wedderburn Burying ground. Formerly covered by a vault. The old stones, Here preserved, were over the entrance door, Having been erected by Sir George Home in 1608. Repaired MDCC'LXIII'P'II."

A small, peculiarly-shaped stone with the death's head in the centre is inscribed :—

"Here lyes the Race of Ancrum. William Ancrum merchant Duns died 1691 Memento mori."

Another small stone has these beautiful lines :—

"Here lies the only comfort of my life,
The best of husbands to a wife.
Great was my loss for his eternal gain,
And hope in Christ that we shall meet again."

---

* Mr. Ferguson.—*Hist. Ber. Nat. Club*, 1890. *Coldingham Letters*, etc. The hospital is also mentioned in Bayamund's Roll.

In the following there is sound logic as well as good gospel truth :—

> "Beneath this stone three infants lie,
>   Say, are they lost or saved?
> If death's by sin, they sinned, for they are here;
> If heaven's by works, in heaven they can't appear.
> Revere the sacred page, the knot's untied—
> They died, for Adam sinned; they live, for Jesus died."

The present church is a handsome modern structure with an elegant tower, in the front of which there is an inscription as follows :—

> "Erected 1790. Destroyed by fire 1879. Restored 1880."

The following is a list of the ministers that have been in Duns since 1568 :—

> John Young—1568 to 1569.
> James Bennet—1581 to 1582.
> Patrick Gaittis—1582 to 1584. After interval of suspension continued to 1611.
> James Gaittis—1607 to 1608.
> John Weemse, M.A.—1613 to 1636.
> Andrew Rollo, M.A.—1637 to 1649.
> Andrew Fairfull, M.A.—1652 to 1661.
> Andrew Collace, M.A.—1663 to 1664.
> William Gray—1666 to 1689.
> Alexander Colden, M.A.—1693 to 1700.
> Laurence Johnstone, M.A.—1703 to 1736.
> Roger Moodie, M.A.—1739 to 1748.
> Adam Dickson, M.A.—1750 to 1769.
> Robert Bowmaker—1769 to 1797.
> George Cunningham—1797 to 1847.
> Henry Scott Riddell—1843 to 1862.
> John Macleod—1862 to 1875.
> Robert Stewart, D.D.—1875 to 1877.
> William Menzies—1878 to 1881.
> William David Herald, M.A.—1882.

The Free Church here was built in 1838 (as a

quoad sacra church). The building is in the Gothic style, with a solid square tower. The present minister is John Miller, M.A., settled in 1868.

The South United Presbyterian Church was built in 1851, on the site of an older one erected in 1752. It is in the Gothic style, but exceedingly plain. The present minister is James Eason, M.A., settled in 1895.

The East United Presbyterian Church is a plain square structure of the meeting-house type, seated for about 500 persons. The congregation (Anti-Burgher) was founded in 1743. The present minister is Alexander John Blair Paterson, M.A., settled as colleague and successor to Rev. Dr. Ritchie in 1891.

Christ Church (Scotch Episcopal) is a neat edifice in the Norman style. In 1852 the Episcopal form of worship was resumed in the town. Two years later Christ Church was consecrated by the Bishop of Edinburgh. The present rector is James Beale, settled in 1878.

Earlston.

The church of Earlston dates from the beginning of the twelfth century, and was at first a chapel dependent on Ederham (Edrom). In the reign of David I. (1124–1153) Walter de Lindsay granted the "Church of Ersildun" to the monks of Kelso, who, in 1171, exchanged it with the monks of Coldingham for the church of Gordon.*

It seems that in early times a HOSPITAL existed here, but only very slight reference is made to it in old records, from which we may infer that it was not of much importance, and it is doubtful if it survived till the Reformation.

The ancient church was demolished and another erected close to its site about the year 1736. This latter has, in its turn, given place to the present handsome church, erected in 1890. Built into its south wall is an old stone, inscribed thus:—

"AULD : RYMRS :
RACE :
LYEES : IN : THIS :
PLACE :"

Tradition says the stone was transferred from the old church (*i.e.*, the building which existed previous to that of 1736). In 1782 the ancient inscription was defaced by some senseless fellow in a drunken

---

* Chalmers' *Caledonia*.

frolic, but the clergyman compelled him to replace it in the same words as before. The effaced characters were very ancient; the present are quite modern.*

Near the Rhymer's stone is another large and elaborately carved stone, with several initials and inscription as follows:—

"I M B
D B   W B"

Below these are carved cross bones, death's head, and two hour glasses, followed by

"I B   W B   M H

"Hic etiam jacet David Brown *de* Park. Qui obiit 5 Decem ætatis 60. Hic Quoq jacet Annabella areskina. Uxor Da. BR. *De* Park Annos 36. Obiit april 6 anno 1681 Aetatis 70.

"Here lyes the body of David Brown of Park who died September 25th 1754 aged 63, in vita dilectus Morteque deploratus.

"Also John Brown of Park his son who died Feby. 3 1813 aged 85."

Near the above stone is another, thus inscribed:—

"Here lyes Master William Brown minister at Nenthorn who deceased the 17 day of November 1692 his age 49; Omnem crede Diem tibi deluxisse supremum."

The church, which occupies a commanding position, was erected on the site of the former church in 1891–1892. It is in the early Gothic style, with a fine tower, and seated for about 700. The open timber-ceiled roof is very effective, and the whole interior produces a singularly pleasing impression of reposeful harmony and beauty.

---

* Mr. Tait.—*Hist. Ber. Nat. Club*, 1866.

There are several seventeenth century stones in the churchyard.

The following quaint inscription appears on a small stone:—

"W B M E 1682
"Althovg my body in the dvst
A litel seson do remen even
Christ y^{ll} rese it vp agene."

On another small stone:—

"Here lys James Aderston in Fans who died March 5 1668 . . . 86 years.
"also Betty and William Brak children to Thomas Brak weaver in Fans."

On a similar stone:—

"Here lyees Thomas Hardie tenent in Hespisshaw who died June 6 1719 aged 64 years."

On an old red stone, whose date is illegible, are the words:—

"Time how short
Eternity how long."

On a stone with date 1782:—

"My Saviour did the grave perfume
In which my dust shall rest
In hope till I my form resume
And be completely blest."

The following lines appear on a small stone:—

"Times glas with rapid course doth run
And makes no stop nor stay
All mortal men prepare should then
Death's sumons to obey."

A small stone is inscribed:—

"Heir lys Johne Broun in Fans Alies Golid [?] who died 4 Sapril 1681 his age 74."*

The communion plate consists of four silver cups. Two bear the inscription:—"For the church of

---

* I am indebted to the Rev. W. S. Crockett, Tweedsmuir, for most of the inscriptions on stones in Earlston churchyard, some of which are now quite illegible. The following additional inscriptions and notes are also kindly supplied by him :—

Within the grounds of Carolside, the beautiful seat of Lord and Lady Reay, is a large flat stone with this inscription :—

"This stone is placed by the directions of Alexander Mitchell Esq. of Stow to mark the spot which was the ancient burial place of the Lauder family."

Some have thought (continues Mr. Crockett) that this idea of Mr. Mitchell's was merely one of his vagaries. But I understand he had good enough reason to believe that where the stone was placed had really been a burial-place, and, in all likelihood, that of the family referred to.

At Mellerstain, in this parish, the burial-place of the Baillie family, the following is inscribed on the tomb of Lady Murray of Stanhope :—

"Here are deposited the remains of Grisell Baillie of Jerviswood, Lady Murray, whose beauty was adorned with every amiable accomplishment, and whose soul was enriched with all those valuable qualities which are seldom united in one character.

"In her an uncommon justness of understanding and firmness of mind, that supported her under the most severe trials, were joined to a constant cheerfulness and sweetness of temper. And whilst the strictest principles of religion, honour, and virtue governed her own actions, they taught her to look with tenderness upon the failings of others. Ever zealous of the service of her friends, dutiful and affectionate to her parents, and bestowing the care of a mother upon the children of her sister, whom she tenderly loved, and who now, unable sufficiently to express what her heart feels, pays this small sorrowful tribute to her memory. She died on the 6th of June, 1759, in the sixty-seventh year of her age."

Earlstoun. 1760." The other two are similarly engraved, but bear no date.

The following is a list of the ministers that have been in Earlston since 1586:—

    James Daes—1586 to 1633.
    James Daes, M.A.—1633 to 1659.
    Henry Cokburn, M.A.—1659 to 1660.
    James Daes, M.A. (reinstated)—1661 to 1673.
    John Hepburne, M.A.—1673 to 1687.
    John Anderson, M.A.—1687 to 1691.
    George Johnston, M.A.—1694 to 1702.
    John Gowdie, M.A.—1704 to 1730.
    John Gowdie—1730 to 1777.
    Laurence Johnston, M.A.—1778 to 1813.
    William Shiels, M.A.—1813 to 1824.
    David William Gordon—1824 to 1868.
    William Mair, M.A., D.D. (present incumbent)—1869.

There is a United Presbyterian Church here. The building is plain externally, but neat and comfortable inside. The present minister is Henry Brown, M.A., settled in 1891.

Eccles.

A CHURCH and nunnery existed here in the early part of the twelfth century. Some authorities have contended that a convent existed at Eccles at a much earlier date, and that it was founded a second time at the above-mentioned period. There is no evidence, however, to bear out this contention.

The munificent Cospatrick, who founded Coldstream, planted a colony of Cistercian nuns at Eccles in 1156, where he endowed a convent, which he consecrated to the Virgin Mary. The nuns of Eccles were at length doomed to feel the sad effects of the disastrous events of the Scottish annals. In 1294-5 Edward I. granted them a protection. In 1296, when the bravest men in Scotland submitted to that overpowering prince, Ada de Fraser, the prioress, with her convent, swore fealty to Edward I., who, in consequence, ordered their estates to be returned to them. Edward II. granted them his protection in 1316-17. After the fatal conflict of Halidon Hill in 1333, the prioress and her nuns found it again necessary to submit to the conqueror; and Edward III. gave them a protection for the house, their people, their lands, and their revenues. In 1523 the chiefs of this nunnery acted the unworthy part of spies for the Earl of Surrey, by informing the English general of the preparations of the Regent Albany for an invasion of England. Albany was thus obliged to raise the siege of Wark, and to retreat across the Tweed to Eccles; and being here falsely informed of the approach of the English army, he decamped at midnight, and hastened to Lauder. In 1544, the prioress and her nuns were involved in the terrible effects of Edward IV.'s courtship of Mary Stewart. On the 27th of September, 1544, the English took the church of Eccles by assault, when they slew within the abbey and town 80 persons, and burnt the abbey and spoiled the village. In September, 1545, the abbey and town of Eccles were again plundered and burnt by the unfeeling Hertford. Marion Hamilton, the prioress, conveyed to Alexander Hamilton, her relation, the village and lands of Eccles; and this unworthy transfer was confirmed by Mary Stewart on the 11th May, 1567. James VI. conferred the estates of this convent on Sir George Home, who was created Lord Home of Berwick on the 7th of July, 1604, and Earl of Dunbar in March, 1605.*

The nunnery appears to have been nearly a square, consisting of about six acres, extending rather further to the south and west than to the east and north.

Some confused ruins of this monastic edifice are to be seen at the west side of the churchyard, and behind the mansion of Eccles House, the east wall of which is evidently ancient, and doubtless formed part of the old nunnery. Two vaulted cells, dis-

---

* Chalmers' *Caledonia*.

playing on the external side of the north wall a blocked, round-headed window, and a small fragment of string-course, with the billet ornament much wasted, are the most noteworthy portions of the remains. A ruinous vault on the north side of the church is also extant. It has two doorways and a round-headed window, all blocked up; but the whole has manifestly undergone considerable alteration at no very distant date, and it is almost impossible to pronounce with confidence upon its primitive features.*

The burial-ground contiguous to these vaults is all paved with fine stones 4 feet beneath the surface, which is a clear proof that there have been many more cells of a similar kind to the former; and as the ground, when turned up, exhibits only a mixture of sand, lime, and earth, it appears to be nothing but the rubbish of the fallen vaults. It is said that the principal entrance to the nunnery was from the west, where there was a very spacious gate, beautifully sculptured, and adorned with a variety of figures. Before the front door of the mansion-house of Eccles, a stone coffin was dug out, above 6 feet long, and covered above with flagstones.†

The church of Eccles seems to have existed some time previous to the foundation of the monastery in 1156. It was consecrated to St. Cuthbert and St. Andrew. While the priory suffered severely in 1545 at the hands of the Earl of Hertford, the

---

* Mr. Ferguson.—*Hist. Ber. Nat. Club*, 1890.
† *The Beauties of Scotland*, by Robert Forsyth.

church was spared, and remained entire till about 1774. It was a Gothic building, in the form of a cross, vaulted and covered with large flagstones, and ornamented with a cross and a very elegant steeple. The building might have stood for many centuries, and it was with the greatest difficulty it was taken down. But as it was too small to accommodate the inhabitants, the proprietors of the parish took it down at the period above mentioned, and built a very handsome modern church on the same ground.*

The building is large and in a good state of repair, and shows no signs of decay, though built 121 years ago. The exterior has much more of architectural design than most country churches built in the latter half of last century; but the interior is bald and uninteresting, and destitute of any single element of beauty or comfort. The tower is considered a very good specimen, and the superior architectural feature lies chiefly in the Norman arches of the windows.

The inscription on the bell is:—

"Feare God yee people of Eckles 1659 I·R."

An excavated sandstone, like a spout or drain, with a corresponding arched stone above it, used in an outhouse, appears to have been part of the piscina of the original church. The font, still in good preservation, is placed in the garden. The bowl is of fine grained sandstone, perforated at the

---

* *Old Statistical Account.*

bottom, and smoothed on the sides, and measures 2 ft. 8 in. in diameter.*

There is preserved in the manse an old hand bell, which would probably be used for funerals and such like, bearing the following inscription:—

"2171 SLEKKE.FO.
HSIRAP · EHT · ROF."

The proper rendering of the above (reading backwards) is:—

"For the parish of Ekkels 1712."

The churchyard has already been referred to. It contains some very old stones, many of which are so weathered as to render their inscriptions quite illegible.

That on a large horizontal stone reads thus:—

"In memory of William Iohnston tenant in Edram Mains who died Novr 3rd 1699 aged 50 years and of Betty Morton his spouse who died Janry 26th 1721 aged 77 years."

A small stone, much broken and defaced, lying flat on the ground, and completely overgrown with nettles and weeds, is thus inscribed:—

"Here lyes Isabel Mason Spouse to Gesper Aire who died 12 March 1687 age 28."

On a very small stone, the upper part of the inscription being illegible, are these words:—

" . . . Wright in Leitholme vho dyed the third day of Jvly 1712 aged 78 as also his sone James liethead who dyed Ivne 15 day 1712 aged 11 years."

---

* Dr. Hardy.—*Hist. Ber. Nat. Club.*

Another small stone is inscribed:—

"Here lyes Agnes Wilson spouse to James Mason Tylior in over mains who died November 20 1699."

A handsome monument, surmounted by an elaborate capital of well-executed carved work, consisting of figures and floral designs, has an inscription, part of which is obliterated, which runs thus:—

" . . . Dickson Antonshil died 15th Augt 1690 aged 75.
"Mrs Elizabeth ker his widow died 12th Novr 1691 aged 68."

At BIRGHAM, on Tweedside, two miles from Eccles, a chapel existed subordinate to the church of Eccles, and was dedicated to St. Mary Magdalene. The churchyard connected with it is still in use for this part of the parish, but no vestige of the chapel building can now be traced.

The stones in the churchyard are much weathered, and there is not much of interest in the way of inscriptions.

A small stone with death's head and hour glass bears the following initials and date only:—

"B D 1683."

The following inscription on a large horizontal stone is almost rubbed out:—

"I W H 1681."

A very small, neatly-carved stone is inscribed:—

"Here lyes Ednem Dods who died the 29 day of March 1699."

A similar stone bears the following:—

"Here lyes John Ingles who died the 20 day of Noumber 1698."

Another chapel, which was dedicated to the Virgin Mary, subordinate to Eccles, stood at the west end of the present village of LEITHOLM. The site of it is marked by an old ash tree, known by the name of the "Chapel Tree," which grows on the summit of the Chapel Knowe. The adjoining ground was used as a place of burial, and is now cultivated. Bones and coffins have been occasionally dug up. Alexander, the parson of Leitholm, was witness to more than one of the earlier charters of Coldstream Priory.

A third chapel dependent on Eccles stood at MERSINGTON, about a mile distant from Leitholm. It is supposed to have been dedicated to St. John. No vestige of this chapel can now be traced.

The following is a list of the ministers that have been in Eccles since 1567 :—

> Robert Franche—1567 to 1596.
> Alexander Home—1608 to 1617.
> Andrew Melville*—1622 to 1622 (a few months only).
> Henry Blyth, M.A.—1622 to 1635.
> John Home, B.D.—1635 to 1649.
> Samuel Douglas, M.A.—1652 to 1652 (a few months only).
> John Jamieson, M.A.—1654 to 1654 (a few months only).
> Andrew Rutherford, M.A.†—1655 to 1660.

---

* Mention is made, under date 1622, of David Home as late minister. Probably he filled part at least of the gap between 1617 and 1622.—Scott's *Fasti Ecclesiæ Scoticanæ*.

† On the 24th January, 1655, a letter was laid before the Presbytery of Jedburgh "complaining of the unrulie and extraordinar actings of some of their numbers (Mr. James Ker of Abbotrule and Mr. John Scott of Hawick), with others, at the pretended admission of Mr. A. R.," when the Presbytery declared against their actings, Mr. John Livingstone of Ancrum dissenting.—Scott's *Fasti Ecclesiæ Scoticanæ*.

John Cook, M.A.—1663 to 1687.
James Balfour, M.A.—1687 to 1691.
John Lauder—1691 to 1729.
Matthew Dysart, M.A.—1731 to 1773.
Adam Murray—1774 to 1794.
James Baird—1797 to 1805.
James Thomson, D.D.—1805 to 1855.
James R. Watson—1848 to 1891.
John Johnston, B.D. (present incumbent)—1891.

There is a Free Church in the village of Eccles—a plain, cruciform structure, erected in 1845. The present minister is Duncan Maclean Black, settled in 1880.

In the village of Leitholm, two miles distant, there is a United Presbyterian Church. It is a plain, barn-like structure, built in 1835. The present minister is John Mitchell Watson, settled in 1879.

Edrom.

The church of Edrom was granted to St. Cuthbert's monks of Coldingham early in the twelfth century by Cospatrick, Earl of Dunbar, and confirmed by David I. in 1139. The gift of Cospatrick was also confirmed in 1150 by Robert, the Bishop of St. Andrews, "in presence of the Synod of Berwick town." Edrom was a vicarage till the Reformation. William De Chatton, "Vicaire de l'eglise de Ederham," swore fealty to Edward I. the 24th of August, 1296.

There were in former times three chapels subordinate to the church of Edrom within the parish —Kimmerghame, Blackadder, and East Nisbet—and outside the parish the distant chapel of Ercheldon (Earlston). Of these four chapels no remains can now be traced.

The chapel at East Nisbet, now called Allanbank, stood on the south-west bank of the river Whitadder, about a mile above the village of Allanton. The site is near a small field still known as the "Chapel Haugh," noteworthy as having been the scene of a Covenanter's conventicle and communion in the persecuting times. The ruins were taken down about the beginning of the present century, and the stones used in the erection of a march dyke between two co-terminous estates in the neighbourhood. The chapel of KIMMERGHAME stood near the Blackadder Water, in a field which to this day bears the name of the "Kirk Park," near Kimmerghame Mill. This chapel, inclusive of a chantry, was conceded by the prior and convent of Durham, between 1233 and 1244, to Herbert de Camera. Between two and three miles farther down the river, and on the same side of it, is the site of the chapel of BLACKADDER, every trace of which has likewise long since disappeared, although portions of the wall which enclosed its burying-ground were standing within living memory.*

The original church of Edrom was of ancient date. It was undergoing repairs in the years 1327, 1333, and 1367 respectively. In 1332 the chancel was newly thatched with straw. The straw and the foreign timber for the work were conveyed from Berwick; the timber unloaded from an "Estland" ship. Bishop Blackadder, who is reputed to have first constructed the Blackadder family vault, was bishop of Glasgow from 1484 to 1508, and it was repaired by Sir John Home of Blackadder in 1696. When the chapel of Earlston acquired parochial privileges Edrom was still its mother church.

There is an interesting and beautiful relic of the old original church of Edrom in the shape of a rounded arch, which forms part of a burial vault of more modern construction. It stands a few yards to the west of the present church. It is all that remains of the twelfth century edifice, and is a fine specimen of the Norman style. Its rounded

---

* Mr. Ferguson.—*Hist. Ber. Nat. Club*, 1890.

shafts, richly carved capitals, and elaborate mouldings remind us of that exquisite sculpture work which, mouldering and fragmentary as it is, still adorns our abbeys.

This arch has evidently formed the main entrance to the earlier structure; and it is most fortunate that it has been preserved, as it is an extremely rich and beautiful example, exhibiting, even in its present decayed condition, some of the most striking and characteristic mouldings of the later Norman style. It is composed of three orders: the intermediate one rising from scolloped imposts, whose abaci are continued a short distance along the wall at each side, and support the outer order; and the inner resting on two cylindrical engaged shafts, with enriched capitals, which are surmounted by square abaci, chamfered below.* The face and soffit of the outer order are embellished with a double embattled moulding, round the outside of which is a narrow band of delicately-carved ornament in very slight relief. The second order displays on both face and soffit a lozenge moulding, embracing on the chamfer-plane a series of large nail-heads, and enriched on the outer face by lines of small pellets. The inner order is chevroned on the face, the soffit being quite plain. The bases of the shafts which support it are about 18 inches below the present level of the ground, and each

---

* In a foot-note Mr. Ferguson observes—"It may perhaps admit of doubt whether the shafts and capitals on which the arch now rests originally belonged to it. They may have formed part of the ancient chancel arch of the church, of which no other portions have survived."

was found, on being exposed, to consist of a round member, slightly moulded, and resting on a square plinth. The day light measures 11 feet by 4 feet 8 inches.*

The appearance of this sculptured doorway in the original fabric would, if anything, be enhanced by contrast with the other portions of the building, for we are informed that as it existed early in the fourteenth century, the roof of the chancel was thatched with straw.†

An addition was built to the church on the south side by Robert Blackadder, archbishop of Glasgow, in the year 1499, of which the greater part is still remaining, though it has been seriously tampered with during the re-building of the other portions of the church. One strong buttress stands out prominently as a monument of the archbishop's "transeptal chapel," as it was called. A large stone built into it is thus inscribed:—

"FOUNDED BY
ROBERT BLACKADDER,
ARCHBISHOP OF GLASGOW,
IN THE YEAR 1499."

Below this is an old heraldic stone bearing the arms of Archbishop Blackadder. It is very much defaced, but on one side can, with difficulty, be traced the initial letter "R" of his name; on the other we can trace the letter "B" quite distinctly.‡

---

* Mr. Ferguson.—*Hist. Ber. Nat. Club*, 1890.

† *Account Rolls of Coldingham Priory, Coldingham Letters*, &c. —*Surtees Society*.

‡ These letters—R. B.—are inscribed on the Blackadder crypt of Glasgow Cathedral along with the Archbishop's arms.

This buttress is surmounted by an old sundial, though it is doubtful if this is as old as 1499. It does not seem sufficiently weathered. Another buttress on the opposite corner has a stone built into it, inscribed thus :—

> " REPAIRED BY
> SIR JOHN HOME
> OF BLACKADDER, BARONET,
> IN THE YEAR 1696."

Below this is another heraldic stone with its characters almost entirely defaced.

The other parts of the church are comparatively modern. It was rebuilt in 1732, and again completely renovated and added to in the Gothic style in the year 1886.

The interior is light and comfortable. The walls are adorned with beautifully-executed scripture texts handsomely mounted, and a large number of marble slabs, inscribed to the memory of members of noted families belonging to the neighbourhood.

The communion plate consists of two silver cups, engraved :—

> "Bought by the Kirk-Session of Edrom for the Communion Table, 1744."

In the churchyard which surrounds the church there are a few interesting stones, the inscriptions on which contain some ludicrous examples of bad spelling.

On a very small stone are these words :—

> "Hir lys the corps of Isbl Kilpatrick who died 11 Dismbr 1712."

On the other side are rudely carved a heart, skull, and bones with "*Memento mori.*"

A medium-sized stone is thus inscribed:—

"Here lyes the body of James Jameson who dyed the 23 day of Novmber 1732 aged 78."

On the other side of this are rudely carved the cross bones and skull, with several implements of industry.

A small, peculiarly-shaped stone bears on one side the words:—

"Here . lyes . the . corps . of . James . Ker . who . died . Desember . 30 . 1719 . and . his . sister . Jane . Ker . who died . Apriel . 14 . 1724."

On the other side is a very small death's head, and some other grotesque figures in human shape, with initials and date, thus:—

"I K   1724   I K."

On a very small, plain stone are these words:—

"Here lyes the corpse of Alexander Scowlar who died January 15 1747."

Another small stone is inscribed thus:—

"Here lyes the cors of William Black who died February 21 1727."

A large upright slab, which has formerly been a horizontal stone, bears a cross or sword in low relief, on one side of which is this inscription:—

"R   B
1676."

A large stone bears these words:—

"Here lyes the corps of Robert Galbraith who died 1669 and Elspeth Johnston his spous who died 1697."

On a small stone we read:—

"Hire lys the corps of Katren Darlin who died Nouember 11 day 1732 aged 19."

The following is a list of the ministers that have been in Edrom since 1574:—

 Patrick Galt or Gaittis—1574 to 1582.
 William Carrail—1583 to 1612.
 Matthew Carraill—1612 to 1646.
 John Home—1646 to 1648.
 William Home—1648 to 1649.
 Thomas Svynetowne (or Swinton), M.A.—1649 to 1661.
 Andrew Bannatin, M.A.—1662 to 1665.
 Alexander Hewat, M.A.—1665 to 1677.
 George Trotter, M.A.—1677 to 1682.
 Patrick Robertson, M.A.—1682 to 1686.
 John Barclay—1689 to 1689 (a few months).
 Andrew Guthrie—1690 to 1698.
 Thomas Anderson—1701 to 1712.
 Alexander Trotter, M.A.—1713 to 1758.
 William Redpath—1759 to 1797.
 John Hastie—1797 to 1822.
 Alexander Cuthbertson—1823 to 1849.
 James Wilson—1849 to 1872.
 George Gibson Gunn—1872 to 1882.
 Macduff Simpson (present incumbent)—1883.

There is a Free Church at the village of Allanton, in this parish, built in 1843—a neat, well-built structure, cruciform in shape, with a pleasing interior. The present minister is Charles Blades, settled in 1887.

Eyemouth.

THERE is very little known concerning the church of Eyemouth. Up till the Reformation it was one of the many dependencies subordinate to the church of St. Mary at Coldingham. The name of Gilbert, the priest of Eyemouth, appears in the year 1295 as witness to a confirmation charter granted by William, Bishop of St. Andrews, to the monks of Durham.

In the year 1340 one Robert de Kellow officiated in the church of Eyemouth. He was soon afterwards raised to the position of sacrist in the priory of Coldingham, but, proving dishonest, he was ejected in 1345. The last of its chaplains was one Thomas Steele.

Of the old original fabric we know almost nothing. The predecessor of the present church stood a little distance to the north. It has been transformed into a modern and well-proportioned dwelling-house, owned and inhabited by Dr. Forsyth, medical practitioner. This gentleman informed the author that, several years ago, while some repairs were being effected, a number of skeletons were dug up, these having been buried below the floor of the church, a practice which prevailed in olden times.

The present church, which was built in the year 1812, is a substantial edifice, but without any claim to architectural beauty. The steeple is high, and forms an admirable set-off against the severe plainness of the building.

The interior is also plain, and after the old style of country parish churches. Several elegant marble slabs, suitably inscribed, adorn the walls. There is a neat pipe organ, which was one of the first to be introduced into parish churches in Scotland. The bell was made in London, and bears the date 1836. It was brought in a sailing smack, was a long time on the journey, and had quite an adventurous voyage. An interesting feature in the building are the beautiful pitch pine joists. These were concealed up till about 20 years ago, when the ceiling was removed.

The communion plate consists of two silver cups, engraved :—

"THIRE CUPS BELONGETH
TO THE CHURCH OF HAYMOUTH
D ^M_S 1689."

The old churchyard is situated about 300 paces north of the church. In one corner is the watch-house, or, as it was called, the "dead-house." It was used in the days of Burke and Hare as a shelter for those who kept watch over the dead, and to guard them against the depredations and violence of the resurrectionists. Though small, it is an exceedingly interesting building, alike for the antiquary and the ecclesiologist. Its walls are composed almost entirely of fragments of old tombstones, many of them bearing elaborate and skilfully-executed carved work. On one stone the date—1680—is observable. Another has 1672.

The tombstones in the churchyard are very much crumbled away and defaced. A large stone built into the back wall is much defaced, and only the following words can be deciphered:—

"C. H. 16 of March 1650."

Alongside of the above is another very large stone, which bears these words:—

"Heir . lyeth . the . bodie . of . Wiliam . Cwrrie . merchant . in . Emowth . who . lived . a . sober . and . christian . lyf . a . haiter . of . al . wickednes . and . sin . died . the . 22 . of . May . 1680 . the . 47 . of . his . aidg."

The following lines appear on a medium-sized stone, erected to the memory of Jean Young 1791:—

"Afflictions sore
Long time I bore
Physicians were in vain
At last it pleased
Almighty God to send
And ease me of my pain."

A small stone is thus inscribed:—

"Agnus Begarny his wife died about the year 1650. Isabel liester wife to And^r Vertue fewer in Eymouth died 28 Octr 1697."

The following is a list of the ministers who have been in Eyemouth since 1615:—

Andrew Ramsay—1615 to 1627.
John Home—1627 to 1646.
James Stratton, M.A.—1647 to 1663.
James Bannatin, M.A.—1665 to 1673.
Gilbert Innes—1673 to ——.
John Wilkie—1677 to 1683.
David Stirling, M.A.—1689 to 1689 (a few months).

James Ramsay, M.A.—1693 to 1707.
John Cuming—1708 to 1715.
James Allan—1716 to 1737.
James Allan, M.A.—1737 to 1767.
Thomas Taitt—1767 to 1776.
James Williamson—1776 to 1785.
George Todd—1785 to 1801.
James Smith, D.D.—1802 to 1825.
John Turnbull (assistant and successor)—1822 to 1843.*
John Murdoch—1844 to 1845.
Stephen Bell—1845 to 1881.
John Dempster Munro (present incumbent)—1882.

The United Presbyterian Church at Eyemouth was erected in 1843. The building is oblong, with pavilion roof. It is after the manner of the old Secession churches, a plain, unpretentious building externally, but neat and comfortable internally. The present minister is David Kinloch Miller, M.A., settled in 1880.

The Evangelical Union Church is a plain oblong building, erected in 1862. The present minister is Thomas Gourlay Taylor, M.A., settled in 1894.

The Primitive Methodist Church is an elongated building, very plain, erected in 1836. The present minister is J. J. Harrison.

The Free Church was erected in 1878. It is a beautiful edifice, with a tall spire, which can be seen a long distance off. The present minister is John Miller, settled in 1887.

St. Ebba's (Episcopal) Church, Eyemouth, was

---

* On adhering to the Protest, joining in the Free Secession, and signing the deed of Demission, Turnbull was declared no longer a minister of this church, 24th May, 1843.—Scott's *Fasti Ecclesiæ Scoticanæ*.

built in 1887. The building is in the Norman style, and occupies a beautiful situation overlooking the bay. Services are provided by the Rector of Christ Church, Duns.

Fogo.

This church was founded about the middle of the twelfth century. In the year 1159 the church of "Foghow," with one carucate of land, was granted by Cospatrick, third Earl of Dunbar, to the abbey of Kelso, in whose possession it remained till the Reformation. David, "vicar of Foghow," swore fealty to Edward I., and thus had his vicarage restored.*

It is not known at what time the church was built. The older part of it, however—viz., the foundations and part of the walls—are undoubtedly ancient. It was completely restored in 1755, when the greater part of the old building was taken down. Two built-up arches, which probably formed the entrance to vaults underneath the church, are distinctly traceable near the middle of the north wall, a little above the level of the ground.

At the east end of the church is the Harcarse aisle, a picturesque and venerable building, completely overgrown with ivy. It has been suggested that this may have been a reconstruction of the chancel of the old church.

A fragment of an old burial slab has been preserved in this aisle. It has carved on its upper

* Chalmers' *Caledonia*.

face an elaborate and ornate cross, with a branched stem, but no portion of the base or arms remains. The work has been unusually well executed, and probably belongs to the fourteenth century.*

An old stone built into the exterior wall of the church, near the south-west door, has sculptured on its outer surface three figures in costume, two men, and a female in the middle, with the following inscription :—

> "We three served God, lived in his Fear,
> And Loved Him who Bought us Dear."

A scroll or sash across the breast of each of the figures is inscribed :—

> "*Vive Memor Lethi.*"

The costume of the figures seems to be that of the Queen Anne or early Hanoverian period. But nothing whatever is known as to whom the figures are intended to represent.

There are several old charters relating to a CHAPEL dedicated to St. Nicholas, which was granted by Patrick Corbet to the monks of Kelso Abbey between 1280 and 1297.† Whether this was a specially endowed chapel in the parish church of Fogo, or a separate ecclesiastical foundation within the limits of the parish, is not altogether certain. The terms of the charters would seem to indicate a distinct foundation; and the double dedication by

---

* Mr. Ferguson.—*Hist. Ber. Nat. Club*, 1890.
† *Liber de Calchou.*

Bishop Bernham (1242 and 1243) confirms this view.*

The exterior of the church is exceedingly picturesque, being almost completely covered with ivy. It stands on the eastern bank of a narrow valley, which leads to a ford on the Blackadder, three miles south of Duns.

The interior of the church is exceedingly plain. On the front of the east gallery are emblazoned the arms of Hog of Harcaise, with initials and motto thus :—

"*Dat Gloria Vires.*
Sr
R.H. 1677"

On a stone inserted in the wall of the Charterhall loft are sculptured the arms of George Trotter of Morton Hall, with motto thus :—

"Deo Dante Florebo, 1671
Mr George Trotter, His Arms."

Fogo possesses an old bowl, which bears the following inscription :—

" x Ex x Done x M x Geo x Troteri x in x W S V M x sacræ x cænæ x in x ecc x Fogensi x Anno x Dom x 1662."

The arms of the donor, enclosed in a wreath, are engraved on the bowl.†

The churchyard contains a number of interesting stones. Built into the churchyard wall is a neat

---

* Mr. Ferguson.—*Hist. Ber. Nat. Club*, 1890.

† Mr. Geo. Trotter was proprietor of Charterhall, in the parish of Fogo. He was an ardent supporter of the Royalist cause, for which he was heavily fined.

stone, bearing the following inscription, which has been restored:—

"Here lies Mr John Pringle minister of the Gospel at Fogo 32 years who died the 22 Feb 1682 of his age the 54 year.

"Clauditur exigua Venerandus Pringlius urna
　　Vir pius et justus, propositi tenax,
Nobilibus prognatus avis prae tuxit avorum
　　Famae, doctrina, religione fide.
Vere evangelicus pastor, Regique Deoque
Fidus erat, patriae spesque decusque suae,
Pauperibus largus patuit domus hospita cunctis
Rebus in incertis certus amicus erat,
Felix innocuum qui sic transegerit aevum
Vivere huic Christus praemia magna mori."

It is stated upon good authority that there used to be in this churchyard a tombstone—though it has not been seen for the last fifty years—bearing the following inscription:—

"Here lyes the body & the Banes
　Of the Laird of Whinkerstanes:
　He was neither gude to rich nor puir,
　But now the Deal has him sure."

Another version of the above runs thus:—

"Here lyes the body and the banes
　Of the michty Laird of Whinkerstanes:
　He had nae other God ava'
　But Rosiebank and Charterha'."

The following appears on a very small stone:—

"Heir lyes Marie . . . Spoos to John Neil who died 1621."

On a neat, medium-sized stone are these words:—

"Robert Paterson who died in Feb. 20 and of his age 78 in the year 1712."

The date 1683, only, appears on a small, plain stone, and on a similar one 1680.

A small, ornamental stone is inscribed thus :—

"Here lyes the body of Jenet Broun daughtr to Thom. Broun heind in Utholm who died the 21 day of Jun 1719 aged 22 years.

"Also Margret his yongest daguhter who died" . . . .

The remaining words of the above are obliterated.

A large, peculiarly-shaped stone bears these words :—

"Her cars and labours ended with her life
Here rests a faithful friend a virteious wife
A daughter anxeious for a mother's fame
With love and reverence this inroles her name."

Below the husband's name, on the same stone, are these lines :—

"An honest man a Peaceful neighbour
A faithful friend to whomsoever."

The following is a list of the ministers that have been in Fogo since 1590 :—

William Methwen--1590 to 1626.
James Methwen—1626 to 1650.
John Pringle, M.A.—1650 to 1682.
William Methven, M.A.—1682 to 1689.
George Moodie, M.A.—1693 to 1721.
William Home—1722 to 1756.
John Todd—1785 to 1814.
George M'Lean—1814 to 1840.
John Baillie—1841 to 1843.
Andrew Redman Bonar—1843 to 1845.
Robert Forrestor Proudfoot—1845 to 1891.
William Henry Gray Smith (present incumbent)—1891.

Foulden.

This is one of those churches about whose origin, unfortunately, there is scarcely a scrap of information to be had from any source whatever. There are two inferences that might reasonably be drawn from such a circumstance. The first is, that its origin may be so remote as to be obscured by the mists of antiquity, a circumstance which would greatly enhance its importance; the second, that, as a religious establishment, co-existent with others of the twelfth century, its ecclesiastical status was comparatively unimportant. To the latter class Foulden, in all probability, belongs.

The living is referred to in the ancient *Taxatio* (1176). "Robert de Ramsay, the parson of Foulden," swore fealty to Edward I. at Berwick on 24th September, 1296, and was soon after reinstated in his former rights and privileges.

It would seem that the priory of Abbey St. Bathans held certain lands in this parish, for in the year 1423-4 Roger Golin, parson of Foulden, disputed the claims of the prioress, and the matter was submitted to the arbitration of the prior of Coldingham. In this parish there is a farm bearing the suggestive name of Nunlands, where it is supposed a nunnery existed in early times, but no record or tradition has been met with that gives any information on the subject. The only fragment in the way of remains which could point to the existence of such an establishment at Nunlands is the basin of an old baptismal font, which was found there a quarter of a century ago.

In the year 1587 the church of Foulden was the scene of an important historical event. A conference was held at which commissioners, representing Queen Elizabeth on the one hand and James VI. on the other, gravely debated the question of Elizabeth's action in the execution of Mary Queen of Scots.

The present church was built in 1786, on what are supposed to be the ancient foundations. It is a plain oblong, each of the side walls supported by three buttresses; the whole almost completely overgrown with ivy, and exceedingly picturesque. It stands on an elevation close to the Duns and Berwick road, five miles distant from the latter, and overlooking a large and beautiful expanse of country on either side of the Tweed. Flodden Hill and a considerable section of the Cheviot range are prominent features in the landscape.

The interior of the church is neat and comfortable. Above the pulpit, at the west end, is a beautiful, stained-glass window in the Gothic style.

Reference has already been made to the basin of an old baptismal font. This remnant of ecclesiastical antiquity lies close to the south wall of the church. It is octagonal in form, with a slightly projecting half-round moulding at each of the angles, and is 27 inches in diameter: the bowl being 16 inches wide by 7 inches in depth, and having a small aperture in the bottom.*

The most interesting tombstone in the churchyard, and certainly one of the most rare antique grave tablets in Scotland, is that which records the decease of the Honourable George Ramsay. It would seem that Ramsay hailed from Fife—" Fyfe fostring peace me bred "—and had a distinguished record in warfare. At length, " Weried with vares and sore opprest," he took up his abode in Foulden, where he seemed to find more peace than on his native soil. The George Ramsay here referred to was the last in the male line of the Ramsays of Foulden, a branch of the family of Dalhousie. It is a large horizontal stone, in good condition. The full inscription is as follows :—

" HEIR . LYETH . ANE . HONORABIL . MAN . GEORG

" Fyfe . fostring . peace . me . bred
From . hence . the . merce . me . cald
The . merce . to . marsis . lavis . led
To . byde . his . battlis . bald
" Weried . with . vares . and . sore . opprest
Death . gave . to . mars . the . foyl
And . now . I . have . more . qvyet . rest
Than . in . my . native . soyl
Fyfe . merce . mars . mort . these . fatal . four
Al . hail . my . days . has . dreven . ovr"

(left margin: His . age . 74.")
(right margin: RAMSAY IN FYLDEN)
(bottom: Baxter . who . departed . jan . 1592 . and . of)

The following appears on a very small stone :—

" Here lyeth Thomas Pentlain who died XXII April 1691."

---

* Mr. Ferguson.—*Hist. Ber. Nat. Club*, 1890.

On another :—

"Here lyes the corps of James William and Euphans who all died betwixt ye years 1705 and 1711."

Another small stone is inscribed :—

"Here lyes the corps of James Thomas Elisbeth Wilsons childer to George Wilson in Edington who departed in the year 1719."

These words appear on a medium-sized stone :—

"Here lyeth Helen Dewar, wife to John Mitchelson older who died 1689.

"Here also lyes John and James sons to John Mitchelson younger John 1689.

"James died 1690."

In a scooped-out panel, on a large horizontal stone, these initials and date are engraved :—

"R S C
1586"

Below this, on the plain surface of the stone, are these initials :—

"R S
E B"

A small, thin stone is inscribed :—

"Here lyeth the corps of Agn . . Bregs wife to John Midelmist who departed this life March the 27 1709 her age 67."

The following is a list of the ministers who have been in Foulden since 1567 :—

David Hume—1567 to 1569.
George Johnston—1572 to 1572 (a few months).
George Ramsay—1574 to 1575.
Thomas Storie—1576 to 1596.
Tobias Ramsay—1596 to ——.

Oliver Colt, M.A.—1614 to ——.
Thomas Ramsay—1630 to 1650.
James Tweedie, M.A.—1652 to 1659.
George Home—1659 to 1660.
David Stirling, M.A.—1660 to 1664.
Patrick Sharpe—1665 to 1681.
Thomas Thomson, M.A.—1682 to 1696.
Robert Park—1699 to 1754.
John Buchanan—1755 to 1785.
David Young, M.A.—1786 to 1812.
John Edgar, M.A.—1813 to 1821.
Alexander Christison—1821 to 1874.
Archibald Bisset—1874 to 1876.
William Campbell, B.D.—1877 to 1883.
John Donald Douglas—1883 to 1886.
John Reid, M.A. (present incumbent)—1886.

Gordon.

In the reign of David I. (1124–1153) the advowson of the church of Gordon was acquired by the monks of Coldingham. These monks in 1171 exchanged the church of Gordon with the monks of Kelso for the chapel of Ersildun and church of St. Lawrence at Berwick. Richard, Bishop of St. Andrews, who died 1177, confirmed to the monks of Kelso the church of Gordon, with entirety of parish of Gordon and of Spottiswood. The diocesan, Gamelin, on 27th May, 1270, granted to the monks of Kelso that the churches of Gordon and Home, which they enjoyed to their proper use, should be served, not by vicars, but honest chaplains and sufficient clerks, for whom he and his successors might be able to answer. In the ancient parishes of Gordon and Westruther, there were of old several chapels. In 1309 the monks of Kelso agreed that Sir Adam Gordon might have a private chapel at any place within the parish of Gordon, with all oblations, yet without a prejudice to the mother church. In return, Sir Adam removed all claim on a carucate of land, with usual easements, in the district of Westruther, which had been granted to those monks by Sir Andrew Fraser, and for which they had agreed to pay two franks yearly.

There was also a CHAPEL at HUNTLEYWOOD, two miles west of Gordon, in the same parish, founded about the middle of the fourteenth century, and dedicated to the Virgin Mary. In old charters it is referred to as " the chapel of the blessed Virgin Mary of Huntlie, commonly called *the Chantory*." It must have continued to exist a considerable time after the Reformation, as it is mentioned as late as 1638. Not a vestige of the building now remains; indeed, its exact location cannot now be ascertained, although a field about a quarter of a mile to the south-west of Huntleywood still bears the name of " Chapel Lea."

At SPOTTISWOOD, five miles north of Gordon, there was also a CHAPEL, which was under the church of Gordon. Its site is now in the parish of Westruther, under which head a fuller notice will be found.

No vestige now remains of the original church of Gordon, which was demolished more than a century ago. The present building, which was erected in 1763, is a low, plain structure, long and narrow, after the good old fashion of ancient churches. A modern wing has been added to the back, and a stone built into it informs us that it was " Erected by Gordon Fewers 1815."

A singular discovery was made several years ago when introducing the heating apparatus into the church; the workmen came upon a pit of about a yard square in the centre of the building, in which 76 skulls were huddled together, and a number of thigh bones corresponding to these, as if they had been removed from some other situation, and deposited there. It was remarked that the skulls were extraordinarily thick, and the thigh bones were acknowledged to be longer than those of the past or present generation. The teeth were wonderfully perfect. Farther along the passage several complete skeletons were found, at intervals, disposed east and west. All these were conveyed to the churchyard for re-interment.

The interior of the church is exceedingly plain. One of the seats, on the authority of the session records, was called the Wedderlie seat, set apart for the Edgars of Wedderlie.

There are two silver communion cups engraved:—

"BELONGING TO THE PARISH OF GORDON 1763."

The churchyard contains one or two stones of minor interest.

On a medium-sized stone which marks the burial place of Thomas Henderson, formerly schoolmaster of Gordon, who died January 13th, 1772, are these lines :—

> " Ah he was great in body & in mind
> A loving Husband & a Father kind
> As he most men Excided in his Stature
> So he Exceled in his Literature
> But although he is gone & greatly mist
> God's will be done we hope he is Blest."

These lines appear at the foot of a modern stone :—

> " He droped like a flower that was nipped in the bud
> He took the repose of the gentle and good
> He blest us he left us our tears they flowed on
> We desire that beautiful land where he is gone."

On a neat and exquisitely carved wooden slab are these pathetic words:—

"Sadly missed."

Appended is a list of the ministers that have been in Gordon since 1574:—

>Archibald Fairbarne, reader—1574 to 1585.
>Thomas Storie—1609 to 1625.
>Francis Collace, M.A.—1625 to 1647.
>Norman Leslie, M.A.—1647 to 1657.
>John Hardie, M.A.—1659 to 1662.
>James Straton, M.A.—1663 to 1682.
>John Findlay—1682 to 1685.
>Thomas Mabane, M.A.—1685 to 1689.
>John Hardie, M.D. (reinstated)—1690 to 1707.
>David Brown, M.A.—1708 to 1726.
>John Bell—1727 to 1767.
>Alexander Duncan, M.A.—1770 to 1800.
>Robert Lundie—1801 to 1807.
>Walter Morison—1807 to 1814.
>David William Gordon—1814 to 1824.
>James Paterson—1824 to 1855.
>William Stobbs, M.A.—1855 to 1885.
>Thomas Porteous, M.A., B.D. (present incumbent)—1885.

The Free Church at Gordon was erected in 1843, and has been repeatedly altered since. It is comfortable and commodious. The present minister is William Adamson MacCallum, settled in 1895.

HUME.

THIS was formerly a parish in Berwickshire, and ceased to have a separate parochial existence in 1640. In the twelfth century the parish included portions of the present parishes of Gordon and Westruther. The church was dedicated to St.

Nicholas, and the patronage belonged to the Earls of Dunbar.

During Malcolm IV.'s reign (1153-1265), Earl Cospatrick gave to the monks of Kelso the church of Hume, with two carucates of land and the meadow called Harestrother within the same parish.*

The chapel of Wederley (now in Westruther parish, and noticed under that head) was in early times under the superiority of the church of Hume.

Concerning the old church building we have no information whatever; only the foundations in the shape of irregular mounds can be traced in the old burial ground of Hume. The only remnant still in existence is an ancient Celtic ecclesiastical bell, 13 inches in length (now in the museum of Kelso). It belongs to the class of bells carried and rung by the hand, and, from its character and shape, to the earliest type of these (the quadrangular-shaped bells in use by the early Celtic church, previous at all events to the twelfth century, as from that time of papal progress in Scotland until the present day, church bells have all been made, or rather cast, in a circular form). This bell has been taken notice of and commented upon by many learned antiquaries in Scotland, and high authorities.†

---

* Chalmers' *Caledonia*.

† It is thus described in the Catalogue of Antiquities, etc., exhibited in the Museum of the Archæological Institute of Great Britain and Ireland, July, 1856, p. 33 :—"An ancient bell of iron, dipped in brass, with which the entire surface was probably coated : its dimensions are almost the same as the Birnic bell ; the form and proportions are identical with those of the *Clogrinny*, or bell of St. Ninian (of which a representation is given).

The site of the church and the burial ground are now included within the parochial limits of Stitchel parish in Roxburghshire. The latter is still in use for the northern part of the parish.

A large, horizontal stone is inscribed :—

"Here lyes George Stevenson tenant in Hume Byers who died 1617.
"Also John Stevenson his son tennant in Hume Byres who died Nov. 1668."

Another horizontal stone has elaborate ornamental carved work and a well-executed cross in relief on its upper surface. No other lettering or date appears on the stone.

A small, ornamental stone is inscribed thus :—

"Here lyes James Broun who liued in Hume and died Septr ye 9 1734 in the 63th year of his age."

A small, round-headed stone, apparently very old, has an ornamental cross engraved on each side, but without any other inscription.

A large, very plain, horizontal stone is inscribed :—

"Here lyes Thomas Trotter tennant in Hume who died August 4 1700 aged 58 years.
" Also his spous Jannet Hoc who died Dec. 15 1721."

This supplies an accurate notion of the fashion of these early Christian relics. The example exhibited was found at Hume Castle, near Kelso. Its previous history has not been ascertained.—The Tweedside Antiquarian Society, Kelso." From the proximity of Hume Castle to the site of Hume church, the inference that the bell belonged to that church is almost fully warrranted.

Greenlaw.

THE church of Greenlaw was given to the abbey of Kelso by Cospatrick, Earl of Dunbar, in 1147, together with the subordinate chapels of Lambden and Haliburton. William Lamberton, who ruled the see of St. Andrews from 1298 to 1328, granted these several churches to the monks of Kelso in consideration of the great waste of the succession war.* In 1296 Nicholas del Camb, vicar of Greenlaw, swore fealty to Edward I.

Of the original fabric of the mother church nothing can now be seen; but the present building, in all probability, rests on its foundations. Previous to 1712 the building, like most of the old churches, was of the long and narrow type, and of rude and primitive construction. At that period it was lengthened and raised to its present height. The style of the building is partly Norman. The corbie-step gables present a feature prevalent in the seventeenth century. At the west end of the church there was erected in 1712 a handsome tower, which forms the principal and most striking feature of the present building. It was erected, not as a church tower or steeple, but as a tolbooth

---

* *Chartulary of Kelso.*

or prison. Its form and style were adopted so that it might at the same time present the appearance of a church tower. It is unique in structure—square, rising to a height of 60 feet, and ending in a corbled parapet top. From this part the steeple proper, which is 18 feet in height, takes its rise, tapering to a point about 78 feet from the ground. The ascent is made by a spiral staircase; and formerly there were small loopholes in the walls. At the foot of this tower is an old iron gate of the tolbooth type; no doubt the original one of 1712. The court-house formerly stood on the west side of the tower. The lower part of the tower, used as a prison, was called "Hell's Hole." There was a grim old rhyme referring to the church and court-house:—

> "Here stands the gospel and the law,
> Wi' Hell's Hole atween the twa."

About forty-six years ago, while some excavations were being made inside the church, it was discovered that there were three floors, and that on the lowest, about 3 feet under the present floor, there have been interments, and are still monumental stones, one of which required to be lifted and removed in excavating a drain.* This stone is still to be seen in the churchyard. It is of oblong form, and has incised upon it a cross, the letters "A. H." in the upper left hand angle, and the letters "I. L." in the corresponding angle at the right hand. The form of the characters shows it

---

* Rev. John Walker.—*Hist. Ber. Nat. Club,* 1863-68.

to be of late date, probably not earlier than the latter half of the sixteenth century.*

There were formerly three chapels in this parish dependent on the mother church—viz., LAMBDEN, HALYBURTON, and ROWIESTONE.

The chapel of Lambden (Lambdene), in the south-east quarter of Greenlaw parish, was built by Walter de Strivelin, who held the lands of Lambden under Cospatrick, about the middle of the twelfth century. Walter obtained from the Bishop of St. Andrews permission to build a church within his village of Lambden, on the concession and request of Cospatrick, the earl, whose fee the said hamlet was.† No vestige of the building now remains.

The chapel of Halyburton was granted to the monks of Kelso in 1176 by "David, the son of Tructe, within his vill, with some crofts and two bovates of land; and all for the sake of the soul of his Lord, Cospatrick, the Earl."‡ In 1261, Philip de Halyburton gave the monks a resignation of the chapel of Halyburton.§ The only vestige of this chapel remaining is a small portion of a wall forming a part of Halyburton farm-house garden wall.‖

The chapel of Rowiestone, the date of whose origin is uncertain, seems to have been connected

---

* Mr. Ferguson.—*Hist. Ber. Nat. Club*, 1890.
† *Chartulary, Kelso.*
‡ *Chartulary, Kelso.*
§ Chalmers' *Caledonia.*
‖ Mr. Robert Gibson, Greenlaw.

with the abbey of Melrose. The building has been entirely removed, but its burying-ground was discovered about fifty years ago, when the field in which it lies was being drained. It was in the form of a square, surrounded on three sides by fine old trees; but so completely, owing to the frequent changes of the agricultural population, had all memory of it been lost, that the original purpose of the enclosure was quite unknown."*

The old bell at present in use in Greenlaw church is inscribed thus:—

"Thomas Brovnfield his gift to the Kirk of Greenlaw Anno 1696 & refounded 1726 R M fecit Edr." Thomas Brovnfield was farmer in Greenlawdean. He "left 400 merks to buy ane guid bell for the paroche church of Greenlaw."

In the front wall of the church is a stone tablet, inscribed:—

"To the memory of Thomas Broomfield, a considerable benefactor to this parish and the public. Buried here Agust 1667. By order of the Kirk Session of Greenlaw this is erected 1742."

Two silver communion cups are engraved:—

"The property of the Kirk Session of Greenlaw 1786."

The churchyard is large, and contains many old stones, the inscriptions on which, unfortunately, are undecipherable. At the bottom of a handsome stone to the memory of William Hislop, surgeon, Greenlaw, are these beautiful lines:—

> "Dear is the spot where loved ones sleep,
>   And sweet the strains their spirits pour,
> O, why should we in anguish weep;
>   They are not lost, but gone before."

---

* Rev. John Walker.—*Hist. Ber. Nat. Club*, 1863-68.

The following is a list of the ministers that have been in Greenlaw since 1606:—

David Home, M.A.—1606 to 1637.
Robert Home, M.A.—1645 to 1673.
John Home—1674 to 1689.
Archibald Borthuik, M.A.—1693 to 1709.
James Gilliland—1711 to 1724.
Thomas Turnbull—1725 to 1734.
John Hume—1734 to 1777.
William Simson—1778 to 1799.
John Stewart—1799 to 1804.
James Luke—1804 to 1820.
Abraham Home—1821 to 1844.
John Hunter Walker—1844 to 1881.
Arthur Gordon, M.A.—1881 to 1886.
Hugh MacCulloch (present incumbent)—1886.

The United Presbyterian Church was built in 1855. It is oblong, with ornamental front and steeplette. The interior is neat and commodious. The present minister is James Ferguson Padkin, settled in 1895.

The Free Church here was built in 1856-7. The first congregation was one of the "Old Light Original Seceders." The church is a neat structure, and it is very comfortable and commodious, with a large hall adjoining. The present minister is Alexander Cameron, M.A., settled in 1875.

Hutton.

This parish consists of the old parishes of Hutton and Fishwick. There is no mention made of the church of Hutton till the year 1243, although in all probability it existed considerably prior to this; possibly in the time of King Edgar, as "Huton" was one of the manors bestowed by that king upon the monks of St. Cuthbert, Durham. In that year the church was dedicated by David de Bernham, Bishop of St. Andrews. In the year 1296 "Thomas, parsona de Huton," swore fealty to Edward I. From this up till the time when Fishwick was united to it in the year 1614 we have no information whatever about the church of Hutton. It would seem that in the year 1655 the church (the original building in all probability) underwent considerable repairs, as the following extracts from session records will show:—

"Dec. 4, 1655.—'Given to George Smith—36 sh.' 'Taken out of the box to pay the woman in Barwick for the timber to the laft—18 sh. starling, 7d.' 'Given to George Smith for thatching of the kirk—50 sh.'"

"Jan. 13, 1656.—'Given to James Scouller in pairt of payment 4 lib. for working the timber of the laft.'"

"Feb. 3, 1656.—'Given out of the boxe to Mrs. Dune in Barwick—8 sh. starling 9d for timber to the kirk.'"

No portion of the pre-Reformation church remains; its successor was built in 1765; this again was replaced in 1835 by the present church —a handsome modern structure in the Norman style, with a fine square tower.*

The churchyard contains a number of old and very interesting tombstones.

An old stone bears the following Latin inscription:—

> "Vixi quoad volui:
> Volui quoad fata volebant;
> Nec mihi vita brevis,
> Nec mihi longa fuit."

On an old, neatly-carved stone:—

"Here lye the bodyes of James King who departed this life 1687 and Janet St—— his wife who died 1672."

On a small stone:—

"Heir lyes John Forman who died in Febrvary 17 1684 and Nicolis Trotter his wife who died in May 21 1694 and James Forman ther sone who died 1700."

An artistically-carved stone bears:—

"Heir lyes Marie Thomson who died in Jvne 27 1698 and Robert Thomson her brother who died in May 10 1693."

---

* When the false alarm about a French invasion under Napoleon was flashed across the country, the Volunteers in the district made Hutton their rallying-point, and spent a night under arms in the old church—i.e., the 1765 structure.—*Rev. Dr. Kirke, Hutton.*

The following appears on a large horizontal stone :—

"HERE WAS BURIED ROBERT HVME OF HUTTON BELL SONE TO GEORGE HVME OF THE NINEWELLS NEPHVE TO THOMAS HVME OF THE BRVMHOVSE PRONEPHVE TO THOMAS HVME OF TINNINGHAME BROTHER TO THE FOUNDER OF DVNGLAS ANNO 1564. AND NICOLAS KER DAVGHTER TO GEORGE KER OF THE HOUSE OF SAMILSTON ANNO 1569. WITH HENRIE HVME THEIR SONE ANNO 1591 AND ISOBEL TOD HIS WIFE ANNO 1578. AND ROBERT HVME IN HUTTON THEIR SONE AND ISOBEL DICKSON HIS WIFE 1618. AND ROBERT HVME SON TO HENRIE HVME IN HUTTON 1678."

On a small stone :—

"Remember man as thou gos by
As thou art now so once was I
Remember man that thou most die."

On a similar stone :—

"Heir lyes the body of Jen Fliman who departed this lyfe in the year 1721 and hir age 18."

On a medium-sized stone :—

" Here is interred the Rev. John Orr episcopal minister of Hutton Parish.
" He was ordained in 1680 and he died in 1694."

The imperfect spelling in the following, which appears on a small stone, is evidently the result of carelessness on the part of the workman :—

" Hear lys the Boy of . . . Dodgle who die 1690 and if his wife 1703."

In the well-kept burial place of the Homes are interred, along with others of that family, the remains of the late

" David Milne Home Esq. L.L.D., F.R.S.E. &c. &c. of Milne Graden, Eldest Son of Admiral Sir David Milne Home G.C.B. Born 22 Janr 1805, died 19th Sept. 1890."

At the base of a neat stone are these lines :—

" Tossed to and fro no more
on life's tempestuous sea
His happy soul hath reached
the shore of calm eternity."

On a very large stone :—

" Heir was bvried John Boomaker 1633 and Margarit Cook his davghter in Law Aprile 24 1668."

In the Hutton Hall aisle—an old burial vault to the west of the church, which appears to be a 17th century erection—there is a stone inscribed :—

" Sacred to the memory of Catherine Home, wife of Robt. Johnston of Hutton Hall, who died Decr 25th 1820 and to her grandchild Catherine Hester Scott who was cut down like a flower of the field Novr 2nd 1823 in the 15 year of her age.
" ' If we believe that Jesus died and rose again even so them also that sleep in Jesus will God bring with him.' May 1831."

The bell in Hutton church bears the following inscription:—

"SOLI · DEO · GLORIA · IOHANNES · BVRGERHVYS · ME · FECIT · 1661."

The above is printed in one circle on the upper part of the bell in beautifully clear and well-preserved, raised characters. The top part above the inscription is decorated with festoon work, the lower part plain.

There was a HOSPITAL at Hutton in early times, but when, or by whom, it was established is not known. It was dedicated to the Apostle John. "Robert de Paxton, prior Hospitalis St. Johannis Jerisolm, apud Huton," and William, the guardian of the hospital, swore fealty to Edward I. in 1296. No traces of the building are now to be seen; indeed, the site cannot now be localised, but it is believed to have stood near the modern mansion of Spittal House. In one of the old Retours it is called Huttonspittal.*

FISHWICK, prior to the year 1614, had a separate parochial existence. The church of Fishwick is very ancient. In 1150 Robert, the Bishop of St. Andrews, in the presence of the synod, which then sat at Berwick, confirmed to the monks of Coldingham the church of "Fishwic." This grant was confirmed by Robert III. (1390-1406). The advowson of the church continued in the possession of the monks of Coldingham till the Reformation.

---

* Mr. Ferguson.—*Hist. Ber. Nat. Club*, 1890. *Retours, Berwickshire, No. 413.*

As already stated, Fishwick was annexed to Hutton in 1614.

The ruins of the ancient church, beautifully situated on the west bank of the river Tweed, nearly opposite the village of Horncliff, were removed about the year 1835, when a mortuary chapel was erected on their site by the proprietor of Broadmeadows. From the brief description given of them in the New Statistical Account of the parish, it would appear that the church had been "a very plain building, long and narrow, and of small dimensions."*

The churchyard of Fishwick is now in disuse, and in a very neglected and dilapidated condition, the stones lying about in great confusion, and the ground overgrown with nettles and long grass.

On a very large horizontal stone is the following inscription, which is much defaced :—

"Here lyes the corps of William Lyle who die 1711 and Helen Boumeker (?) his spous who Diod 1702 . . ."

On a similar stone :—

"Heir was bvried Georg Maben 1612 and William Maben his sonne departed first of September 1666."

On a very small stone :—

"I · C · 1642
M · S · 164-."

Another large horizontal stone bears :—

"Heir was bvried Christian Lyle anno 1648 and John Hutscheson her husband 1661."

---

* Mr. Ferguson.—*Hist. Ber. Nat. Club*, 1890.

On a similar stone :—

"I P.
E R 1654."

The following, on a large horizontal stone, is almost illegible :—

" 158 . .
I I S
G I
H I."

Another horizontal stone bears :—

" Heir · lyes · William · Wilson · 1656 · and · Robert · Wilson · his · sone · 1677 · and · Margie · Blekiter · his · wife · 1675 ·

" Here · lies · William · who · deceased · the ·" (there is a sudden break here ; the words have evidently been omitted).

" And · Allison · King · his · spous · who · deceased · the ·" (another break here).

The following inscription, on a horizontal stone, is executed in a beautifully ornamental style :—

" Heir lyes the body of John Wilson who died 1690 and Helen Aird His spous who died 1699 and John Wilson Grandchild who died 1716."

Another horizontal stone, with grotesque and rudely-executed sculpture work, bears :—

" Heir was bvried John Hogard who died Anno 1640."

The spelling in the following is amusing :—

" Here lays the boody of Beatrich Grac spows to Peeter . . . who departed this lyfe Novembr the 2 1705."

On a very small stone :—

" Mary Brovn 1647."

The words on a stone which bears some elaborate sculpture work are these :—

"Here lyes John Bald who died 1679."

The following is a list of the ministers who have been in Hutton since 1571 :—

    John Clapperton—1571 to 1576.
    John Home—1578 to 1585.
    William Methwen—1585 to 1586.
    Archibald Oswald, M.A.—1586 to 1594.
    Thomas Storie—1596 to 1597.
    Alexander Lumisdene, M.A.—1599 to 1607.
    Thomas Ogiluy—1607 to 1608.
    John Weemse, M.A.—1608 to 1613.
    Allan Lundie, M.A.—1614 to 1636.
    James Lundie—1636 to 1649.
    Patrick Hume—1649 to 1679.
    James Orr—1680 to ——.
    Gilbert Lawrie, M.A.—1693 to 1727.
    Robert Waugh[*]—1730 to 1756.
    Philip Ridpath—1759 to 1788.
    Adam Landels—1789 to 1821.
    John Edgar, M.A.—1821 to 1858.
    Robert Kirke, D.D. (present incumbent)—1858.

---

[*] There was great opposition to the ordination of Waugh. The service had to be conducted under protection of the Sheriff, with upwards of a hundred military, although the doors of the church had been barricaded.—Scott's *Fasti Ecclesiæ Scoticanæ.*

Ladykirk.

The parish of Ladykirk comprehends the more ancient parishes of Upsetlington and Horndean.

The church at present in use is a very interesting one, and, though of no great antiquity, has a peculiar and very romantic origin. As the story goes, James IV., when crossing a ford in the Tweed near by at the head of his army, was in danger of being swept away by the swollen current. While in this plight he prayed earnestly to the Virgin Mary for deliverance, and vowed that if he should be saved he would build a church in honour of "Our Lady." The erection which sprang up in fulfilment of this vow was called Ladykirk.

The church is cruciform in plan, and consists of an aisleless nave with a tower at the west end, a chancel with a semi-hexagonal termination, and north and south transepts, or transeptal chapels, similar in form to the chancel. Internally the nave measures 41 feet 8 inches in length, by 23 feet 3 inches in width; the chancel is 36 feet long, and of the same width as the nave; and the internal projection of the chapels is 15 feet 10 inches, and 16 feet 4 inches, respectively. The style of the architecture, as might have been expected, is far from pure, and displays the strong leaning to

First-Pointed forms so characteristic of Scottish Gothic in its latest phases. The walls are ornamented with nineteen buttresses, on the top of which are carved figures, some of them now much worn by time and want of due care. Two string courses are carried round the building a short distance above the basement, the upper one rounded above, the lower sloping, and both hollow or concave below. A slightly projecting cornice, with a hollow on the under side, runs along the top of the wall beneath the eaves.

The windows are mostly plain, lanciform openings, divided into two pointed lights by a nominal branching at the top, an exception being the east window of the chancel, which is wider than the others of this form, and is divided into three lights by two monials branching and intersecting in the head. The three principal windows in the south wall, however, are different in style, being wide, depressed-segmental or elliptical-headed apertures, each containing three pointed lights. The exterior window jambs have, in every case, two outer plain-chamfered orders, and an inner or tracery order hollow-chamfered. The interior jambs consist of a plain splay, with a quirked edge-roll carried up round the rear arch. Over every window, except one in the north wall of the nave, is a label or dripstone, terminating at each side in a rudely-sculptured head.

Entrance has been provided to the interior by three doorways, the principal one being at the west end of the south wall of the nave. It is round-headed; the jambs are composed of two continuous filleted rolls, with a wide hollow between; and the upper string course before described is carried round the head as a dripstone. The day light measures 8 feet from the ground to the crown of the arch, and is 5 feet in width. Another doorway of smaller dimensions, leading into the chancel through its south wall, displays in the jambs a single, continuous, filleted roll, the dripstone as in the first-mentioned example being merely a continuation of the upper string course round the head. The third, which is in the north wall of the nave, is now concealed on the outside by a building recently erected to contain the heating apparatus of the church. There is a blocked doorway in the wall of the south transept, but it is evidently quite modern.

The tower is of four stages, each of the three lower vaulted internally, but undistinguished on the outside except by small, rectangular, chamfered openings in the west face. The upper stage is modern (1743), and is surmounted by a kind of four-sided dome, with a belfry above, altogether out of harmony with the rest of the edifice. A wide, square-headed doorway, on the west side of the tower, affords access to the interior of the lowest or ground stage; and an assent to the upper stages is provided by a newel-stair, placed in a turret occupying the angle between the north wall of the tower and the west wall of the nave.

The aspect of the interior of the church, though not wanting in impressiveness, is singularly bald. It has a pointed vault, the plainness and barrenness of which are only partially relieved by a series of transverse ribs in the nave and chancel, and of shorter diagonal ones at its eastern and lateral extremities, all of them broadly chamfered, and resting on moulded corbels. The arches opening into the transepts are of two chamfered orders, rising from capitaled responds with mouldings of debased character. These, however, are wholly restorations, although they may probably be exact reproductions of the original work. The superincumbent walls are carried above the roof outside, and form gables which terminate the roofs of the transepts at their inner extremities—a very unusual, if not altogether unique, feature.*

On the interior western gable is a marble slab inscribed :—

" D. O. M.
Hanc ædem beatæ Virgini Mariæ
  Sacram ab inclyto
Jacobo quarto Scotorum rege
  anno post Christum natum
M.D. Extructam at deinde
  temporis vetustate accolarumque
incuria collapsam etiam
pene ruinis involutam Jam tandem
fundi parochialis domini, sua
pecunia instaurandam curarunt
Denique campanili addito gulielmus Robertsone a Ladykirk
orandam curavit.
  MDCCXLIII.
Restituta MDCCCLXI."

---

* Mr. Ferguson.—*Hist. Ber. Nat. Club*, 1890. Mr. Ferguson's description of the architectural features of this church is given here at considerable length. It possesses a special value in this case from the fact that Ladykirk was one of the last pre-Reformation churches erected in Scotland, and is still substantially unimpaired.

LADYKIRK. 143

The latter date, 1861, refers to the renovation of the church—clearing out the partitions and furnishings of the portion used as the parish school, cleaning the entire walls, reseating, and heating. Immediately under the Latin inscription is a brass plate with the following inscription from the pen of the late Lady Marjory Marjoribanks of Ladykirk :—

"The clock in the tower of this church was given by the Right Honourable Marianne Sarah Robertson Baroness Marjoribanks of Ladykirk in grateful remembrance of, and thankfulness for many mercies and blessings vouchsafed to and enjoyed by her during her possession of the estate, and also in thankful commemoration of the 14th day of October, 1881, when, amidst a wind storm of unusual severity, disastrous in its effects to persons and property both on sea and on land, and appalling to all people, a merciful Providence was graciously pleased to protect this parish and its inhabitants, by the preservation of human life within its bounds. 1882."

A curious old oak chest stands in the south transept, richly carved, and bearing inscriptions on its upper surface and on one side. Round the top margin are these words :—

"It is more blessed to give then too receive. Gods worst is better than the worldes best."

On the inner surface, forming the two longer sides of a rectangle, are the words :—

"Saynt Nycholas."
"Liverpool."

In the central space enclosed by the rectangle is the following :—

"Man · shal · not · live · by ·
Bread · alone · but · by · everic ·
Worde · that · procedeth · out ·
Of · the · mouth · of · ye · lord."

On the front side along the upper margin :—

"16 | Edward Williamson's gift to ye trulye poore and aged of ye Psh | 51."

Along the lower margin :—

" My trust is in God alone."

In the space between these marginal readings :—

" I was hungrie and ye gave me meat. I was thirstie and ye gave me drink. A stranger and ye tooke me in, naked ye clothed me. I was sick and ye visited me."

This old oak chest was placed where it now stands in Ladykirk church on 23d October, 1885, as a gift from the Lady Marjoribanks of Ladykirk. A year or two elapsed, when suddenly a lengthened correspondence sprang up (having its origin at Liverpool), in magazines and by letter, between the churchwardens of St. Nicholas Church, Liverpool, and the Rev. William Dobie, minister of Ladykirk. *The Antiquary, Liverpool Mercury,* and even *The Scotsman* had a hand in the discussion which arose as to whether the chest was the "original" or a mere "copy," and no definite conclusion has, as yet, been arrived at. The subject has in the meantime dropt. The churchwardens at Liverpool and *The Antiquary* think the venerable chest is "a lie in oak," and should be burnt. Visitors are divided in opinion, while the minister of Ladykirk thinks, be it the original or "a modern antique," it is worthy of being preserved, and he intends to do so, were it only because it was purchased for, and gifted to this church by the now deceased Lady Marjoribanks of Ladykirk, whose memory he cherishes with sincere affection.

Upon an inlaid stone, inserted in the exterior wall above the chancel door, there is the following inscription :—

"D. O. M.
"Jacobus Scotorum quartus rex teudam.
Tuto quum transuisset hanc ædem votam
Mariæ Virgini ad deum unum solumque
Spiritu veritateque colendum milesimo
Quingentesimo annoque jubilæo fundavit."*

There are pits on the freestone wall of Ladykirk church which some attribute to the effects of the weather, others to stray missiles from artillery of Norham Castle; the latter is not at all improbable.

In the churchyard there is nothing as yet disclosed that can be considered remarkable. The older stones are so weathered as to render it quite impossible to decipher the inscriptions.

---

* "The above record," says the Rev. William Dobie, minister of the parish, "is not older than the present (19th) century."
The same authority says :—"There is evidence above the main south door, on the outside, that a tablet had been inserted there at some time, but the tablet, with whatever it might have told, has long ago entirely disappeared; while on the outside, and directly above the north door, and looking to Scotland, there is similar evidence that a tablet had been once placed there, and tradition has it that the Royal arms of Scotland, decorated with the Order of the Garter, were carved on that now lost stone. It is not disputed that Henry VII. of England did compliment James IV. of Scotland with the Order of the Garter, and in the then circumstances of both kings nothing was more appropriate, as James was about to marry Margarita Henrici nata major filia—an event which took place on the 8th August, 1503, and in its consequences was so important as, in the third generation, to unite the two crowns of England and Scotland in the year 1603."—*Hist. Ber. Nat. Club.*

These lines appear on a large stone erected to the memory of two children :—

> "Ere sin could blight or sorrow fade,
> Death came with friendly care,
> The opening bud to Heaven conveyed,
> And bade it blossom there."

On a small, plain stone, the oldest legible, is this inscription :—

"Here lyes the body of Patrick Blair who died November 7 1738 his age 37 years."

The ancient parish of UPSETLINGTON, now included in Ladykirk, probably existed in the 12th century, although we have no mention of it until the year 1296, when "Henry de Strivelin," parson or rector of Upsetlington, swore fealty to Edward I. at Berwick. In the year 1327 Abraham Crichton was rector of Upsetlington. The supplementary treaty of Chateau Cambresis, entered into between Francis and Mary, King and Queen of Scotland, and Elizabeth, Queen of England, was signed on 31st May, 1559, in the ancient church of Saint Mary of Upsetlington.

About a quarter of a mile north of the hamlet of Upsetlington is the site of the "Rectoria de Upsetlington," or, as it is written in the tax roll of St. Andrews, "Saint Mary's Church of Upsetlington." About half way down the declivity to the lip of the Tweed lies the only remnant of the rectory—a block of stone, squarish, weather-worn—fit memorial of the *to Kuriakon*—*i.e.*, the something that belonged to the master; now prostrate, but enduring still.*

---

* Rev. William Dobie.—*Hist. Ber. Nat. Club.*

Near the site of the ancient village of Upsetlington there existed in early times a well called St. Mary's well, the water of which still ripples into the ravine below. A memorial in the shape of a watering trough for cattle was erected near the spot about the beginning of the present century by the then proprietor William Robertson, Esq., which bears the inscription—" Well of St. Mary of Upsetlington." A short distance from this stands a square modern pillar, upon a platform, about ten feet high, inscribed " Ann's Well."

The ancient parish of HORNDEAN was also included in this parish. The church or chapel of Horndean is mentioned about the middle of the 12th century. " William de Vetereponte" acquired the manor of Horndean during the 12th century. He transferred the church of Horndean to the monks of Kelso. The grant of Vetereponte was confirmed by Bishop Hugh, who ruled the diocese of St. Andrews from 1177 to 1188.*

In the Pontificale Ecclesiae S. Andrews, among the churches dedicated by David de Bernham, Bishop of Saint Andrews, we find " Eccl. de Hornerden" eodem anno (1243) 4th April (dedicata).†

There was also a HOSPITAL founded at Horndean during the 12th century. Robert Byset, who owned the manor of Upsetlington on the Tweed, founded in the reign of David I. (1124–1153) a hospital, which he dedicated to St. Leonard at

---

* Chalmers' *Caledonia*.
† Rev. William Dobie.—*Hist. Ber. Nat. Club.*

Horndean. The master of that hospital witnessed a charter of Hyde de Simprine during the short reign of Malcolm IV. (1153-1165). Robert Byset granted this hospital with its pertinents to the monks of Kelso, on condition that their abbot should keep a chaplain there; and should maintain in it two poor persons, whom the donor and his heirs should have the right of placing therein. At the end of the 13th century those monks had, at Horndean, this hospital, with 16 acres of land, a fishing in the Tweed, and a park within the manor of Upsetlington, for which they thought themselves obliged to support a chaplain for celebrating divine service in the hospital chapel, and to maintain two paupers under the pious donation of Byset.*

No trace whatever is left of the hospital of St. Leonard, in the same parish; but the charter by Robert Byseth, Lord of Upsetlington, conferring it on Kelso Abbey, indicates that it stood between Horndean and the Tweed—*juxta Twede ex opposito de Horwerden.*†

Horndean ceased to be a separate parish about the year 1576.

The old burial ground of Horndean stands in the centre of an open field within about 200 paces of the Tweed. It is surrounded by a low broken-down wall. There are about a score of old stones confusedly scattered about in a sadly neglected condition, sheep and cattle having free access to the place. Unless some means are speedily adopted

---

* Chalmers' *Caledonia*.
† Mr. Ferguson.—*Hist. Ber. Nat. Club.*

to protect the few sacred memorials, these, it is greatly to be feared, will soon entirely disappear.

Owing to their ruined and fragmentary condition, only one seventeenth century stone has its inscription (and that only partially) legible. It is a large horizontal stone with these words :—

"Heir · lys · George · Bell · 1663 · and · Besi · Brekentn · his · wife · 1658."

On a very small stone :—

"Heir lais the body of Gorg Park ci who died Meay 17 and Brak who deid Mearch 2 1745."

On a medium-sized stone :—

"Here layes the body of Peter Brown who died March 16 1749 His age 28 years."

A small stone, with the most beautiful and exquisitely chiselled sculpture work, is inscribed :—

"Heir · lyes · the · corps · of · Willeam · Cunningham · mason · in · Horendon · who · died . March · th 3 · 1758 · his · age · 50 · years."

On a small stone :—

"Here · lyes · the · body · of · Mergret · Cunningham · spous · to · William · Frisken · who · died · May · th 12 · 1743 · aged · 61."

These words, on a very small stone, are almost illegible :—

"Here lyes the body of James Henderson who deid Apr. . . 1716."

The following is a list of the ministers that have been in Ladykirk since 1576 :—

Andrew Winsister—1576 to 1585.
John Home—1607 to ———.
David Hume, M.A.—1635 to 1650.
William Craufurd, M.A.—1651 to 1690.
William Gullan—1694 to 1697.
Samuel Kilpatrick, M.A.—1697 to 1711.
George Ridpath, M.A.—1712 to 1740.
John Todd—1741 to 1786.
Thomas Mill—1788 to 1800.
George Todd—1801 to 1819.
George Home Robertson—1819 to 1842.
William A. Corkindale—1842 to 1845.
John Stevenson, D.D.—1855 to 1859.
William Dobie (present incumbent)—1859.

At Horndean there is a United Presbyterian Church built in 1786, and enlarged in 1812. The present minister is James F. G. Orr, M.A., settled in 1896.

Langton.

The church of Langton is ancient. During the reign of David I. (1124–1153) the manor of Langton, with the advowson of the church, belonged to Roger de Ow, a Northumbrian follower of Prince Henry. Roger de Ow granted to the monks of Kelso the church of Langton. From him the estate passed to William de Vetereponte, or Vipont, who continued to these monks the church with its tithes and lands. In 1296, John, vicar of Langton, swore fealty to Edward I. at Berwick, and had his rights restored.*

In the year 1684 the church seems to have been in such a condition as to require no repairs, the report of the commissioners at the parochial visitation of that year, called by order of the Bishop of Edinburgh, while Patrick Walker was minister, having been satisfactory. At the next visitation in 1700 the Presbytery are said to have found "several things necessary to compleat ye same," and the moderator, by their appointment, "recommend ye persons concerned to see to ye repair y^r of." At the third visitation in 1721 they discovered that "the roof was in ill condition," and in 1727

---

* Chalmers' *Caledonia*.

it fell to the ground. It then underwent thorough repair, and stood till the more modern edifice was erected in 1798 at the village of Gavinton, half-a-mile from the old site.*

In the old, and now disused, burial-ground at Langton there is what seems to have been the chancel of the church, long since converted into a

---

* Here is a sworn statement, made by the then minister and others, showing the state of the church and parish in 1627 :—

"At the kirk of Langtoun the eight day off Junj 1627 yeiris Mr Samuel Sinclar Minister thair and with him, &c., &c.

"Imprimis the number off communicantis foure hundreth and fyftie and formetymes fyve hundreth the parochin is off thre mylles off lenth and one off bredth. The Kirk standis almaist in the middes off the paroch quhair thair is the greittest confluence off pepill duelling twa myllis from the remotest pairt on the on syd and a myll distant from the remotest on the other. This kirk wes neuir vnited. It is ane auld kirk off the abbacie off Kelso. Sir William Cockburn off Langtoun knight patron to the vicarage of Langtoun since the tyme off reformatioun. The ministeris stipend is five chalderis cherittit victuell off Louthiane mett twa pairt ait meill thrid pairt beir with the viccarage off the parochin quhilk is thus vplifted. Sir William Cokburn of Langtoun knicht he payes tuentie pund to the minister for the viccarages of his haill manissis Johne Cokburn vncle to the said Williame he vpliftes the rest of the vicarage of the paroch by ane Inueteratt possession and payes nothing for it. The Minister possesses and vpliftes the vicarage off syne roumes to wit Chouslie Ladyflat Greitrig Quhithill and Craes and the teind hay off the rest of the parochin except off the Laird off Langtoun his manissis befoir exceptit. Item the minister vpliftes ten merkis as feu maillis off the vicaris landis quhilk hes bein in vse to have bein payit to his predecessouris vicaris of Langtoun be the gudman of Chouslie titular to the vicaris landis.

"The Minister his stipend is payit be the Abbottis or Lordis off Kelso.

"There is no hospitallis nor foundatioun for them nor chaiplainries prebendaries nor freir landis within the parochin so far as we knaw."—*Reports on the State of Certain Parishes in Scotland.*

burial-vault, 22 feet wide by 20 feet long externally. It is situated a little to the south-east of Langton House. At the west end of this vault, and projecting about a foot laterally, there is a small fragment of what must have been the north wall of the nave; but the whole bears evident marks of having been repeatedly altered, and probably not one original detail is left. The east elevation contains two small round-headed windows of apparently seventeenth century date, 6 feet apart, each 27 inches high by 14 inches wide.*

There are a number of old stones in the burial-ground at Langton, but the place is in a wretched condition, so overgrown with nettles and long rank grass that several of even the tall stones are completely overgrown and hid from view.

On a very small stone only the date 1656 is legible.

The following appears on the upper surface of a small, clumsy stone:—

"James Lamb 1671."

On a similar stone:—

"Hear lyeth James Watherston who died 12 of Janwavr 1712."

A small, neatly-carved stone bears:—

"Hear lyes Jean Cvrriie who dyed March 21 1707 and James Cvrrie who dyed Febr. 6 1708. Son and daughter to Robert Cvrrie."

A tall, very slender stone is inscribed:—

"Hir lys Alexander Wer 1620."

---

* Mr. Ferguson.—*Hist. Ber. Nat. Club*, 1890.

The date 1605 appears on a stone of most elaborate and artistic design. The other part of the inscription is defaced beyond recognition.

On a small, thick stone :—

"Adam Gallway of years was 81 yet to this world of them was dead 11 Feb 1683."

Within a square pannel of a richly-carved stone :—

"John Cockburne 1686."

On a small, plain stone :—

"Here lies Wiliam Bour (?) and James Lovri his son 1710."

In Langton Wood, opposite Hainingrig, there is the site of a nonjurors' chapel, which was erected in 1676, but no vestige now remains.

The church at present in use was erected in 1872 as the successor of, and on the same site as, that which was erected in 1798. It is a neat building in the Gothic style, with a handsome tower. The interior is light and exceedingly comfortable. At the west end above the pulpit is a beautiful, stained-glass window.

The stones in the churchyard are all comparatively modern.

These lines appear on a medium-sized stone :—

"The rosebud droop'd
But free'd from sin and toil
May bloom afresh in more
Congenial soil."

On a similar stone :—

"One by one we cross the river.
One by one we're passing o'er.
One by one the crowns are given
On the bright and happy shore."

LANGTON. 155

The communion plate consists of two silver cups, engraved:—

"DAVID GAVINUS DE LANGTON NUPER APUD MIDDELBURGUM IN ZEALANDIA MERCATOR ECCLESIAE DE LANGTON DONO DEDIT. ANNO DOM : MILLESIMO SEPTINGENTESIMO SEXAGESIMO PRIMO."

A curious old relic in the shape of a hand-bell is still preserved. It was probably used as a death-bell. It bears the inscription:—

"FOR JOHN GALLAVA IN LANTUN 1685."

The following is a list of the ministers that have been in Langton since 1585:—

John Home—1585 to 1586.
William Methwen—1586 to 1595.
James Gaittis—1596 to 1607.
Samuel Sinclair, M.A.—1607 to 1653.
John Burne, M.A.—1659 to 1672.
Robert Happer—1677 to 1681.
Luke Ogle, M.A.—1679 to 1682.
Patrick Walker, M.A.—1682 to 1689.
John Dysart, M.A.—1691 to 1694.
John Dawson, M.A.- 1698 to 1726.
James Dawson, M.A.—1727 to 1733.
James Laurie, M.A.—1734 to 1757.
David Johnston—1758 to 1765.
Andrew Smith—1766 to 1789.
Alexander Girvan--1789 to 1809.
John Brown*—1810 to 1843.
David Dunlop—1844 to 1864.
Robert Stormonth Darling—1864 to 1867.
James L. Blake—1867 to 1892.
John Peattie, M.A.—1892 to ——.

---

* Brown, on joining in the Free Secession, was declared no longer a minister of this church, 20th June, 1843.—Scott's *Fasti Ecclesiae Scoticanae*.

Within a short distance of the parish church is Gavinton Free Church, a neat building, erected in 1843, altered and improved in 1884. The present minister is Johnstone Walker, M.A., settled in 1880.

Lauder.

THE church of Lauder existed at a period not later than the middle of the twelfth century. During the reign of David I. (1124–1153) the advowson of the church belonged to Hugh Morville, who enjoyed from that king almost the whole of Lauderdale. Malcolm IV. (1153–1165) confirmed to the monks of Dryburgh "terra illa quam *kisth*, clericus, tenuit de avo meo de ecclesia de Cadisleya," and the chapel of St. Leonards, and these chapels—Kedslie and St. Leonards—were subordinate to Lauder as the mother church. In 1268, through his wife, Devorgilla, a descendant of the De Morvilles, it came into the possession of John Baliol, who resigned it to the monks of Dryburgh, in whose possession it remained as a vicarage till the Reformation. In 1296, William Fitzaleyn, "le clerc de Laweder," swore fealty to Edward I. at Berwick.*

In this church, in 1482, the Scottish nobility held their famous conference, which resulted in the seizure of James III., and the murder of his favourites, who, as old Pitscottie says, were hanged "over the bridge of Lather befoir the king's eyes." Both bridge and church have long since been

---

* Chalmers' *Caledonia*. *Chartulary of Dryburgh*.

demolished. The latter stood on the north side of the town, facing Lauder fort, which now forms part of Thirlestane Castle.*

Reference has already been made to two chapelries subordinate to Lauder—the CHAPEL OF ST. JOHN, near Kedslie, and that of St. Leonards. The former stood on the west side of the Leader, five miles south of Lauder, and the place still bears the name of Chapel-on-Leader. As already indicated, this chapel existed in the reign of Malcolm IV. (1153-1165). Further than this we have no information about its history.

The CHAPEL OF ST. LEONARDS stood about two miles directly south of Lauder, and a mile north of the village of Blainslie. Its churchyard is still in existence, but, sad to relate, only a solitary fragment of a tombstone remains. Its elegant design is still traceable, and part of the inscription as follows :—

" . . . 1733. As also Thomas Darling his grandson who deperted this life the 16 of July 1747 aged 22 years."

What appear to be the foundations of the chapel are dimly traceable, and measure 60 feet long by 40 feet wide.

In addition to the chapel there was also a HOSPITAL at St. Leonards. There is a building here, which is occupied as a farm-house, part of which appears to be very old, and the walls are nearly 4 feet thick. It is just possible—highly probable, indeed—that this formed part of the

* Mr. Ferguson.—*Hist. Ber. Nat. Club*, 1890.

hospital building. There are two stones built into the south wall, one of which is inscribed thus:—

"Trivno A M H Deo Gloria."*

The other stone, which forms the lintel of a window, bears the following:—

"☞ Devs . est . fons . vitae.
"I . thrist . for . the . vater . of . lif."

The present church, which is situated in the centre of the town of Lauder, was built in 1763; since then it has undergone frequent repairs, the last of which was in 1820. The building is cruciform, each arm of the cross being equal. The dome rises from the centre, and rests on four arches, which are built of red freestone—at present covered over with plaster. Originally there seem to have been no windows except in the end gables, and these are of considerable size, and are semi-Gothic, in harmony with the arches on which the dome rests. The windows in the side walls which have been inserted at a later date, and also those under the larger windows in the gables, are square, and give the whole a mixed architectural appearance. The church is large and commodious, being seated for 750.

---

* It is the opinion of Dr. Hardy, than whom there is no one better qualified to form a correct judgment, that the initials "M. A. H." are those of Master Andrew Home, "Pensionary and Rector of Lauder, who secured the property for himself and his illegitimate son William, when Dryburgh Abbey was dissolved."

The bell is a very large one, and is said to hold six bushels. It bears the following inscription :—

"Given by Charles Maitland, his Majesty's treasurer depute 1681. John Milne Fecit Edin^{r.} recast by James Earl of Lauderdale out of the vacant stepends 1751 and recut again 1834."

There are two communion cups (the gift of the notorious Duchess of Lauderdale), engraved with the Lauderdale and Murray arms. Two silver flagons have, in addition to Lauderdale and Murray arms, the following inscription engraved on their lids :—

"A GIFT TO THE CHURCH OF LAUDER AUGUST THE 10TH ANNO DOMINI 1677."

The following entry appears in kirk-session records :—" Lauder, 1677, Nov. 3. This day there was presented to the Minister two Cuppes with covers and two Flagons, all of silver, with keepers of leather sent in Guift from my Lady Duchess of Lauderdale for the use of the Church of Lauder."

In the churchyard there are many handsome stones, besides a few old and interesting ones.

An old stone, built into the back wall of the churchyard, whose inscription is so weathered as to be almost illegible, bears date 1671, and the following lines :—

> " Here lyes interred ane honest man,
> Who did this churchyard first lie in ;
> This monument shall make it known
> That he was the first laid in this ground.
> Of mason and of masonrie,
> He cutted stones right curiously.
> To heaven we hope that he is gone,
> Where Christ is the chief corner-stone."

Another stone in the churchyard wall is inscribed:—

"Here lys the body of Master Thomas Mabone minister of the gospel at Gordein thereafter Schoolmaster of Lauder who died the 12 day of Febr Anno Dom 1711 his age 58.

"Here lys also the body of Isabel Home spous to the said Mr Mabone who died the first of Aprile 1708 age 54.

"With Thomas and Grissall Mabons their children."

On the back of an old stone is another version of the familiar lines:—

"Stop passenger as you pass bye
As you are nou so once was i
As i am nou so you must be
prepare prepare to follow me."

On a small stone:—

"N T　M H　J R　I B

"George Renwick s Burying place who hath been in Europ Asia Africa."

There is elaborate sculpture work on the other side of this stone.

The following is a list of the ministers that have been in Lauder since 1567:—

Ninian Borthwick —1567 to 1574.
William Frank—1574 to 1576.
John Knox, M.A.*—1576 to 1582.
Alexander Lauder, M.A.—1584 to 1613.
James Burnet, M.A.—1615 to 1636.
James Guthrie, M.A. —1642 to 1649.
William Johnstone, M.A.—1652 to 1659.
David Forrester, M.A.—1661 to 1684.
John Lumsden, M.A.—1685 to 1689.
William Abercromby, M.A.—1693 to 1697.

---

* Knox was grand-nephew of the great Reformer.

Andrew Duncanson, M.A.—1700 to 1706.
George Logan, M.A.—1707 to 1718.
Thomas Pitcairnes—1720 to 1835.
James Lindsay—1736 to 1746.
Robert Fisher—1747 to 1753.
James Ford, M.A.—1753 to 1810.
Peter Cosens—1811 to 1845.
William Smith—1845 to 1858.
Donald Macleod—1858 to 1862.
James Middleton, M.A.—1862 to 1874.
A. B. S. Watson, B.D.—1875 to 1876.
Thomas Martin, M.A. (present incumbent)—1876.

The Free Church was erected in 1843. The building externally is very plain, but internally one of the most pleasing and comfortable. The present minister is Duncan Turner, settled in 1882.

The United Presbyterian Church is a plain structure of moderate size, erected in 1841. The present minister is Thomas Keir, M.A., settled in 1885.

Legerwood.

THERE is evidence of the existence of a church at Legerwood in the early part of the twelfth century, John, priest of "Ledgaresude," having been one of the witnesses to a charter granted in 1127 by Robert, bishop of St. Andrews, in favour of the priory of Coldingham. It would seem, shortly after this, to have come into the possession of the abbey of Paisley. Walter, son of Alan de Lauder, granted the church of "Legerwode," with its pertinents, to the monks whom he brought from Shropshire to Paisley. Subsequently this grant was confirmed by Malcolm IV. (1153–1165), and also by his successor, William I. (1165–1214). The church continued with those monks, who served the cure by a vicar till the Reformation. Walter, vicar of Legerwood, swore fealty to Edward I. at Berwick, 28th August, 1296. On 30th May, 1453, Thomas de Fersith, vicar of Legerwood, obtained from the English king a passport for three years to visit, as a pilgrim, the shrine of the apostles.*

The original edifice, of which no inconsiderable portion still remains, was built in the Norman period, probably not later than 1130. It has con-

---

* Chalmers' *Caledonia*.

sisted of a nave and a narrower and very short chancel. The nave, which is about 50 feet long by 27 feet wide externally, has been used as the parish church since the Reformation; but a series of repairs and alterations, the first of which seems to have been executed in 1717, with the usual disregard to the original character of the building, has completely obliterated every early feature except the chancel-arch, which, although blocked up and otherwise disfigured, is apparently quite entire. So far as the details can be seen, it appears to consist of two semi-circular orders, each square-edged on the side next the chancel, but on that next the nave moulded into a wide quarter-hollow and half-round. On the same side are visible two bearing-shafts in each jamb, having cushion-capitals, with square abaci chamfered below, and adorned on their faces with a band of the sunk star ornament, which is continued along the wall at each side of the angles. The same ornament appears, arranged in square panels, and with slight variations of form, on most of the capitals themselves, one notable exception being that of the inner pillar of the north jamb, which displays on the outer face a peculiar engrailed or reversed scolloped ornament of a somewhat inartistic type. The outer capital of this jamb has a rude kind of knob, or volute, on the angle immediately below the abacus. On the opposite jamb, the half of the inner capital has been cut or broken away to make room for a hat peg! The shafts rise from round bases, convex in profile, and resting on square plinths, which are covered by the soil. The width

of the arch, measured between the extremities of
the jambs, is fully 15 feet; the height from the
bottom of the plinths on which the shafts rest to
the top of the imposts is nearly 8 feet, and from the
imposts to the crown of the arch 5 feet.*

The chancel, which is now exterior, and forms
the Moristoun burial-aisle, is roofless, and its walls
have been considerably reduced in height. Many
of the original details, however, are left, and these
are interesting. In each of the four corners there
is a massive projecting shaft, which, in all probability, supported the groin ribs of the vaulted stone
roof. There are traces of two old windows, one of
which is situated about the middle of the north
wall, and the other in the east elevation. They
are narrow and round-headed, and bear indications
of rich artistic design. Other ornamentations
appear on different parts of the walls, all of which
seem to be of Norman date, and testify to the
genuine antiquity of this part of the building. In
this aisle is the tomb of John Ker of Moristoun and
his wife, that noble heroine, Grizel Cochrane. It
was she who robbed the postman near Belford of
the warrant for her father, Sir John Cochrane of
Ochiltree's, execution. Sir John was leagued with
Sir Patrick Home of Polwarth in the political
troubles of the reign of James VII. By this means
she succeeded in delaying her father's execution
till successful intercession was made for his life.

The tomb consists of a handsome monument with
massive pillars on each side. It contains the arms

---

* Mr. Ferguson.—*Hist. Ber. Nat. Club*, 1860.

of Ker of Moristoun, with the date 1691 in bold characters, and the initial letters "I. K.," one on each side.

The inscription on the slab runs thus:—

> "HER RESTS THE CORPS OF JOHN KER OF MORISTOUN WHO DEPARTED THIS LIFE THE 27 OF SEPTEMBER 1691 IN THE THRETIETH YEAR OF HIS AGE. "AS ALSO THE CORPS OF GRISSELL COCHRANE HIS LADY WHO DIED THE 21 OF MARCH 1748 IN THE 83D YEAR OF HER AGE."

The following appears on the same stone, and has been recently re-lettered:—

> "THE GRISSELL COCHRANE HERE REFERRED TO IS THE SAME WHO SO HEROICALLY SUCCEEDED IN SAVING THE LIFE OF HER FATHER THE HONBLE SIR JOHN COCHRANE OF OCHILTREE 2ND SON OF THE 1ST EARL OF DUNDONALD THEN UNDER SENTENCE OF DEATH AT EDINBURGH OWING TO HIS CONNECTION WITH THE POLITICAL TROUBLES OF 1685."

On a large, very plain horizontal stone, lying flat on the ground, appears in large letters the first of the above inscriptions.

Built into the exterior wall of the Moristoun aisle, on the east, is a neat memorial tablet, inscribed thus:—

> "Here lyes Sibela Hume spouse to John Moffat of East Moristoun who died the 10 of October 1719 aged 71 years."

Another memorial stone, built into the same wall, has its inscription almost completely obliterated.

A very small stone in this wall bears in very illegible characters the letters:—

" M
R   Y
1767."

The church interior is somewhat after the old-fashioned style. The seats are bare and uncomfortable, and the paved stone passages impart to the place a feeling of coldness, unrelieved by the dullness and monotony of bare walls. It is well lighted and lofty. The old Norman arch already referred to is an object of special interest alike to the antiquary and ecclesiologist. The exterior of the building is plain. There is an old stone built into the front wall, on which are inscribed some characters which are so confused as to be quite undecipherable. A stone built into one of the walls is inscribed:—

"Repaired 1717."

Another stone in the front wall states that it was

"Repaired 1804."

There is an interesting old sundial attached to one of the corners of the church, and inscribed thus:—

"M
W   G
1682."

The communion plate consists of an old cup, inscribed:—

"THE GIFT OF M^{RS} JEAN TROTTER RELICT OF Y^E REV^D MR WILLIAM CALDERWOOD 1717, LATE MINISTER OF Y^E GOSPEL at LEGERWOOD."

In this parish in early times there was a lazar-house, or HOSPITAL, dedicated to St. Mary Magdalene. It is supposed to have been founded by Walter, son of Alan de Lauder, who obtained this manor from Malcolm IV. (1153–1165). In 1296 Nicol de Lychardeswode, the chaplain, guardian of the hospital at Lychardeswode, swore fealty to Edward I., and, no doubt, had his forfeited revenues restored.*

The hospital was situated at "Auldenestun," and belonged to the abbey of Melrose. There is a charter relating to it in the Melrose *Chartulary*, entitled "Carta leprosorum de Moricestun." This would seem to indicate that the hospital was in the neighbourhood of Morriston.†

In the churchyard the most noteworthy stone is that which commemorates the Rev. William Calderwood. It is a handsome stone, richly ornamented with elaborate carved work along the sides, and resting on six pedestals about 3 feet high. The inscription runs thus :—

"Here . lyes . that . pious . and . faithfull . servant . of . Jesus . Christ . the . Reverend . M^r . William . Calderwood . who . was . admitted . minister . of . this . parioch . of . Ligertwood . June . 12, . 1655 . where . he . laboured . in . the . work . of . the . Gospel . till . he . was . turned . out . for . not . conforming . to . Prelacy . an . 1662 . an^d . then . he . frequently . tho . privately . visited . that . Parioch . till . the . Episcopal . minister . was . turned . out . that . he . returned . to . his . work . Septr. 8, . 1689 . and . continued . therein . till . his .

---

* Chalmers' *Caledonia*.
† Mr. Ferguson.—*Hist. Ber. Nat. Club*, 1890. *Liber de Melrose*, &c.

death . which . was . June . 19 . 1709 . being . the . 81 . year . of . his . age . and . the . 54 . of . his . ministry.
 "This monument was put up by his Relict Jean Trotter.
 "Repaired by some of the Parishioners 1838."

Another large and finely-decorated horizontal stone is thus inscribed:—

"Here lyes William Montgomry of Makbichill who deceased the 9 day of December 1689 his age 63 years.
 "Repaired by the Right Honble. James Montgomery Lord Chieff Baron of the Court of Excheqwer the grandson of the above Wm Montgomery 1798."

The following appears on a medium-sized stone:—

"Hire : lays : James : Graham : leat : tennant : in : Thornidick : who : died : Aprile : 26 : 1758 : aged : 66 : years : also : Janet : Pringle : 15 : 1770 : aged : 61 : years : also : Androw : & : Janet : Grahams : there : grand : children :"

Over the grave of a very young child is a neat wooden slab with these beautiful lines:—

"The Lord He gave and He will take,
So blessed be His name,
We'll bear it all for Jesus' sake,
The Lamb who once was slain."

The following is a list of the ministers of Legerwood since 1592:—

David Forsyth—1592 to 1593.
George Byris, M.A.—1593 to 1640.
Thomas Byris, M.A. (assistant)—1634 to 1653.
William Calderwood, M.A.—1655 to 1662.
Thomas Byres, M.A. (reinstated)—1666 to 1682.
Gideon Broun, M.A. (colleague)—1666 to 1676.
William Layng, M.A. (colleague and successor)—1677 to 1689.
William Calderwood, M.A. (reinstated)—1689 to 1709.
James Campbell, M.A.—1711 to 1714.
Thomas Old, M.A.—1717 to 1737.
Walter Douglass, M.A.—1738 to 1752.

William Gullan—1753 to 1792.
Robert Scott—1793 to 1795.
James Baird—1795 to 1797.
James Young*—1797 to 1798.
Henry Garnock—1799 to 1811.
George Cupples—1812 to 1833.
John Hunter Walker—1834 to 1844.
James Macnair—1844 to 1853.
James Langwill—1853 to 1859.
Archibald Brown—1859 to 1891.
William Rankin (present incumbent)—1891.

---

* Young was licensed by the Presbyterian class of South Northumberland in 1782, was minister of Kirkly and Glanton respectively, and admitted to Legerwood in 1797; his settlement here was rescinded by the General Assembly in 1798, he not being qualified according to the laws of the Church. This decision so affected his spirits that he died of a broken heart at Coldstream, 23d January, 1799.—Scott's *Fasti Ecclesiæ Scoticanæ*.

Longformacus.

THIS parish is made up of the two old parishes of Longformacus and Ellam, united in 1712. We have no information bearing on the foundation and early history of the church of Longformacus. From the 13th century till the Reformation the barony, with the advowson of the church, was held in succession by Morthington of Morthington, the Earls of Moray, the Earls of Marsh, and a branch of the St. Clairs of Roslin.* This is about the extent of the information, meagre as it is, that we possess of this church until the year 1730, when it was rebuilt upon the old foundations. From the old and weathered appearance of portions of the walls, it has evidently been built from the materials of the older church.

It was renovated in 1892, and, during the excavations in the interior of the old building, the workmen came upon large quantities of bones. There was also unearthed a large sepulchral stone with a cross sculptured upon it, which, in all probability, is very old. It is now placed in the vestibule of the church. On a projecting stone in the exterior back wall there is an old sundial, which bears no date, and which is probably a relic of the 1730 construction, or it may be, earlier.

---

* Mr. Ferguson—*Hist. Ber. Nat. Club*, 1890.

Near it is a portion of the chain and a small fragment of the collar which formed the *jougs*. This relic is now rarely to be met with in old churches.

It is a pretty little church inside, with apse and chancel, and beautifully stained-glass windows. Inserted in the south wall is a sculptured stone bearing the St. Clair arms, with the letters I. S. above.

There is nothing very remarkable in the churchyard, the inscriptions on the older stones being so much defaced.

This inscription appears on a small stone :—

"Here lyse James Robertson who dyed Janwary the 9 1734 aged 25 years."

On another small stone :—

"Hear lies the body of James Trotter and Elisabeth Litter his wife."

The following, in the most rudely printed and somewhat obscure characters, appears on a very small, peculiarly shaped stone :—

"Heir leys James Shir L men (?) to Jeneat Hwem who deprted on Janwary 27 day 1707."

There are two communion cups inscribed :— "Given by Sr Robert Sinclair of Lamformacus to kirk thereof 1674."

In the centre of the village, about 50 yards from the church, is a "holy well," dedicated to Our Lady, with date 1581. On the stone work above the spring is an elaborate monogram containing the letters D. W. B. (David Wardlaw Brown, proprietor of Longformacus).

The following is a list of the ministers who have been in Longformacus since 1594:—

>   John Douglas, M.A.—1594 to 1607.
>   George Rowlle, M.A.—1607 to 1652.
>   Thomas Wolfe, M.A.—1668 to 1671.
>   Alexander Douglas, M.A.—1672 to 1677.
>   John Broun, M.A.—1678 to 1684.
>   Robert Smyth, M.A.—1684 to 1714.
>   Daniel Sinclair, M.A.—1715 to 1734.
>   Robert Monteith, M.A.*—1735 to 1776.
>   Selby Ord—1777 to 1814.
>   George Bell—1815 to 1830.
>   Henry Riddell—1830 to 1843.
>   Walter Weir—1844 to 1871.
>   George Cook, M.A., B.D.—1871 to 1891.
>   James Johnstone Drummond, M.A., B.D. (present incumbent)—1891.

The Free Church stands in the centre of the village of Longformacus. It was erected in 1847, and is in the form of a cross. The present minister is George Taylor, M.A., settled in 1870.

ELLEM, as already stated, was a separate parish up till 1712. Concerning its history we know almost nothing. The church was dedicated by Bishop Bernham in 1243. Thomas Brown, the parson of Ellem, swore fealty to Edward III. after

---

* Monteith was a volunteer, and his bravery in that capacity has been thus sarcastically described in the witty ballad of "Tranent Muir":—

> "Monteith the great, when hersell shit,
> Un'wares did ding him o'er man,
> Yet wadna stand to bear a hand,
> But aff fou fast did scour, man."
> —Scott's *Fasti Ecclesiæ Scoticanæ.*

the battle of Halidon Hill (1333), and in return received protection for his person and his parsonage.*

The remains of the old church are situated on an elevation on the north bank of the Whitadder, close to Ellemford, about three miles above Abbey St. Bathans. The foundations are easily traced, and a small portion of the south wall is still standing.

The churchyard has evidently been very small. Only two or three stones are lying about in confusion.

On a large horizontal stone :—

"Here lyeth James Scovgal in Eel . . . who died the 5 of Nov. 1627 of his age the 75 years.
"*Me mento mori.*"

On a similar stone :—

"Heir lyeth James Scovgal who died in 25 day 1691."

The following is a list of the ministers of Ellem from 1567 till its incorporation with Longformacus :—

        Robert Flint, Reader—1567 to 1585.
        Matthew Liddell—1585 to 1591.
        Robert Levingstoun—1593 to 1595.
        James Gaittis—1595 to 1596.
        George Reidpath, M.A.—1596 to 1627.
        Robert Home, M.A.—1635 to 1645.
        Patrick Home—1649 to 1650.
        William Home—1652 to 1653.
        Zacharias Wilkie, M.A.—1654 to 1683.
        John Brown, M.A.—1684 to 1713.

---

* Chalmers' *Caledonia*.

Mertoun.

THE church of Mertoun existed about the middle of the twelfth century. It was given by Hugh de Morville to Dryburgh. In 1241 the church was consecrated by Bishop de Bernham. Dene David Dewar was vicar of Mertoun in 1483. Having laid claim to the abbey of Dryburgh, a lawsuit ensued as to the validity of his claim. It came before the Lords, and they, in 1488-9, found that Dewar, being a spiritual person, and the abbacy litigious, the abbot ought to summon him before the spiritual "judge."*

The present church of Mertoun dates back to 1658. Since that time it has undergone many repairs. An old stone which forms the outer step at the east entrance is inscribed :—

"I V L I E 1658."

On a modern stone, above this door, is the same inscription; while another stone above the west door bears the following :—

"Rep^d 1820."

The building is long and narrow, and exceedingly plain.

The bell bears date 1762.

In the front wall still hangs the old chain complete, and part of the collar of the *jougs*.

---

* *Parish Records.*

The east gable is completely covered with ivy, which, with the neat belfry at the opposite end, and the whole snugly embowered within the leafy shade, imparts to the little church a decidedly picturesque appearance.

In the interior there are five old-fashioned square pews belonging to the heritors: one worthy of special notice is that belonging to the Right Hon. Lord Polwarth, which is enclosed with wood to the height of 5 feet, and has in it an old-fashioned fire-place.

The site of the original church of Mertoun is about a mile distant in the centre of the churchyard, still the parish burial-ground. The east wall of this church still stands to a height of about 8 feet, and portions of the north and south walls still remain. The building has been in the Norman style, although all trace of its architectural features have disappeared.

An old sepulchral slab, bearing an ornamental cross carved in relief upon its upper surface, stands near the south wall. It bears the marks of considerable antiquity, but no date or inscription of any kind appears on it.

The churchyard contains a considerable number of very interesting stones.

On a very plain stone much defaced:—

"James Mill 1693."

On a small stone dated 1771:—

"A budding rose swept doun
By water overfloun
Like a plant of renoun
A sweet flour tho wnrloun (?)"

On a small, very plain stone :—

"A L March 17 I L 1691."

On a stone to the memory of John Lockie are these lines :—

"Patient was he in his distress
Unto his parents dear
To serve in glory was his hope
And learning was his care."

On a small stone :—

"Hear . lys . Alexander Lockie . who . died . the . 15 . day . of . Agos . 16 . 95 . His age 54."

On another small stone :—

"Here Lays George Halliburton tailer in Ne . . . who died feb 15 1713 aged . . years."

On a tall, narrow, and very peculiarly shaped stone :—

"Heir lyis the Body of ane Honest man John Haitley who died the 25 day of January 1698 His cag being 58 years."

On a very small stone :—

"Here lyes Bessey Gregg spoues to John Beety who died the 10 of March 1699 & of age 40."

DRYBURGH ABBEY.—In this parish are the ruins of that ancient and far-famed monastic establishment. Dryburgh is the queen of Scottish abbeys, enjoying the calm solitude of undisturbed repose away from the busy haunts of men. Here it stands embosomed amid the shadow and gloom of wood on the left bank of the Tweed, which, by a majestic sweep, surrounds it on three sides. It would seem as if nature here had usurped the domain of art, for not only are the ruins largely overgrown with ivy, but from heaps of masonry the spruce and the holly may be seen flourishing, and even from the higher portions of the building trees have sprung up and attained considerable growth.

The abbey was founded in 1150 by Hugo de Morville.* As early as the sixth century, however, a monastery existed on the spot. St. Modan, who was one of the first Christian missionaries in Britain, was abbot of Dryburgh about the year 552. Its name also points to the probability that in early times a Druidical establishment existed on the site of the present ruin. Though now a mass of crumbling walls and tottering arches, yet in its very wreck and decay the grey pile towers up in solemn grandeur as a venerable remnant of a long-past and almost forgotten age.

Entering at the north-east corner, we have the high altar on the left, towards which the monks and abbots reverently knelt and bowed in silence. From the high altar to the west door is a distance of about 230 feet—this includes the choir and nave. Passing through the west door, and proceeding southward, the dungeons—three in number—are reached. They are damp and dingy, as such places usually are.† Their size is about 30 feet long, by

---

* Authorities differ as to the real founder of Dryburgh; some, even good authorities, maintain that it was due to David I., but the balance of evidence seems to go in favour of Hugo de Morville.

† It was in one of these that, about 150 years ago, an unfortunate female wanderer took up her abode. It is said that

12 feet broad, and 9 feet high. One of these communicates with the cloisters at the north-west corner. This is a courtyard of considerable extent, and adorned on all sides with objects of elegantly-carved mason work. It measures about 100 feet square, and is tastefully laid out in the form of a lawn. South of this, and entered from the south-west corner of the cloisters, are the cellars, a cluster of commodious chambers, including the old wine and almonry cellars, and above these is the refectory, or great dining-room of the monks, the walls on the west and south of which are now almost completely gone. This apartment measured 100 feet long, by 30 feet broad, and 60 feet high. Proceeding eastward, we enter the library, and, north of this, the abbot's parlour, adjoining which is the chapter-house, an elegant and richly-adorned chamber measuring 47 feet long, 23 feet broad, and 20 feet high, enhanced at the east end by five Early English Gothic windows, and at the west end by a large circular-headed centre window, with a small one on each side. The hall is ornamented with a series of intersected arches. North of the chapter-house is the family vault of the Biber Erskines,

---

during the day she never left her dismal dwelling, but when night came she issued forth and sought the hospitality of the neighbouring residents, returning, hermit-like, to her miserable abode precisely at twelve o'clock. By the more intelligent class she was looked upon with compassion, while she was regarded with some degree of terror by the vulgar. It is believed that she adopted this strange mode of life as the result of having taken a vow, that, during the absence of her lover, she would never look upon the sun. He, alas! never returned, having fallen in the wars of the '45 rebellion."

adjoining which is St. Modan's chapel, and, underneath, the family vaults of the Erskines of Dryburgh and the Earls of Buchan. To the northwest of the high altar is that part of the north transept, St. Mary's aisle, in which are the three vaults—burial-places of the Haigs of Bemersyde, the Haliburtons of Mertoun, and the Erskines of Sheilfield. Sir Walter Scott was buried here on 26th September, 1832. The spot is therefore hallowed and honoured by the dust of "the mighty minstrel." In life he loved to linger amid the calm solitude and tender beauties of the place, and here also, now that his tongue and pen are still, his ashes rest in peace and undisturbed repose far from the "madding crowd":—

> "So there, in solemn solitude,
>   In that sequestered spot,
> Lies mingling with its kindred clay
>   The dust of Walter Scott!
> Ah! where is now the flashing eye
>   That kindled up at Flodden Field,
> That saw, in fancy, onsets fierce,
>   And clashing spear and shield?
>
> *   *   *   *
>
> "The flashing eye is dimmed for aye;
>   The stalwart limb is stiff and cold;
> No longer pours his trumpet-note
>   To wake the jousts of old.
> The generous heart, the open hand,
>   The ruddy cheek, the silver hair
> Are mouldering in the silent dust—
>   All, all is lonely there!"

What still remains of this vast structure is sufficient to give a fairly accurate conception of the architecture and general design; and these leave nothing to be desired in the way of beauty and perfection of style and workmanship. It is, indeed, a study of the highest interest alike to the architect and the archæologist, having been founded at the time of the transition from the round-headed Norman arch to the Early English or pointed arch. That much of the original work still remains is evident from the numerous details of a transitional character to be met with throughout the ruins. The interior of the chapter-house is one of the most notable examples; for here we have the interlacing Norman arches, the intersection of which is supposed by some authorities to have given rise to the pointed arch of later times. Of the further development of the Early English style, a good example is seen in the fine circular window, locally known as St. Catherine's Wheel. The font, which now stands in the chapter-house, is evidently older than any part of the building, and may, without much hesitation, be ascribed to either the tenth or eleventh century. In the various arches are represented no fewer than four different styles—viz., the Roman arch with square sides, the deep-splayed Saxon, the pillared and intersected Norman, and the Early English Gothic pointed arch.

The western doorway is a masterly and unique piece of work, consisting of a semi-circular arch composed of richly-moulded ribs of shafts springing from the ground and running round the arch without a break, with rosettes placed at regular intervals in the deep hollows, the effect of which is peculiar, and yet highly pleasing. This doorway, however, requires to be seen before it can be fully understood and appreciated.

Of the once magnificent fabric little now remains but the mouldering fragments of a noble specimen of ancient art. But the story of its sadly checkered career comes down to us fresh and imperishable, full of inspiration, from the example of the old monks whose lives' work lay within its sacred walls.

Its surroundings lend an added charm to the place. Close by is

"Tweed's fair river, broad and deep."

Encircling it are the majestic trees, with their long deep shadows adding darkness to solitude, the soft rich turf decked with sweetly-scented wild flowers in great profusion—a fairy scene worthy indeed of the poet's rapturous words:—

"Hail, Dryburgh! to thy sylvan shades all hail!
As to a shrine, from places far away,
With awe-struck spirit, to thy classic vale
Shall pilgrims come to muse, perchance to pray;
More hallowed now than in thy elder day,
For sacred is the earth wherein is laid
The poet's dust; and still his mind, his lay,
And his renown shall flourish undecayed,
Like his loved country's fame, that is not doomed to fade."

At different periods the abbey suffered severely at the hands of the English. In 1322, Edward II., returning south, pillaged and burned it; and again, in 1385, Richard II. subjected the sacred edifice to the flames. In 1545, also, a similar fate befel it, being plundered and burned by an English force under the Earl of Hertford. Thus the present building is but the surviving elements, the mere wreck, indeed, of a once splendid monastic edifice, in which the master hand is discernible. It has passed through many hands, and is now the property of the Biber Erskines.

The churches held by Dryburgh Abbey were Mertoun, Channelkirk (with its chapels Glengelt and Carfrae), Lauder (with its chapels St. John at Kedslie and St. Leonards).*

A stone bearing the following inscription is built into the chancel wall :—

"Erected to the memory of Hugo de Morville Lord of Lavtherdale and Lord High Chancellor of Scotland who founded and bvlt this abbey vnder King David I. he died in 1162."

Near by is another stone with the following :—

"Here lyes Adrian Haig who died being the time of my Lwdek Powstatic this is the trwth : His espovseric : Margarat Hwtly sister of the Hwrdlaw 1630.

"Dauid Haig died Jwly 4 1752 : aged 85 also his spows Agnns Sciruen who died : Octb^r 20 1754 Aged 84 years.

"Also Here lies Andrew Haig, who died the 29th January 1649."

Another of the same family is thus commemorated :—

"Here lies Andrew Haig . . . in Dryburgh who died the 1st of December, aged 60 years also Jane M'Mellan, his wife, who died the 4th December, aged 70 years ; both in the year of our Lord 1671.

"As Jonathan and Israel's king
In love did still abide,
So pleasant were this happy pair,
Their death did not divide."

---

* In an enclosure, still called the Chapel Field, about a mile west of the ruins of Dryburgh, were found in 1788 the remains of a place of worship, concerning which there is no record more than the tradition of the name of the field.—*Annals and Antiquities of Dryburgh*, 1828.

The following lines were written for the above, but were not allowed to be put on the stone :—

> " O cruel death, for ever killing,
> Has killed poor Haig and Jean M'Mellan ;
> But still in hopes that they shall meet,
> They laid poor Jean at Andrew's feet."

These stones are situated near the *ultima domus* of the Haigs of Bemersyde.

On the tomb of Sir Walter Scott are these simple words :—

"Sir Walter Scott, Baronet. Died September 21, A.D. 1832."

On a large stone built into the wall at the foot of the bell stairs a large cross is engraved in the centre, and these words round the margin :—

" Hic Jacit Honorabilis vir Adam Robson de Gleddiswood, qui obiit vii Octobris, Anno Domine 1555.'"

The oldest stone in the abbey with legible inscription has these words :—

" M. Alexander Simpson, æcclesae apud Mertonis, obiit 17 Julii 1639.

> " Whose life and happy death
> This sacred stone records,
> By Christ's blessing and passions,
> Still resting in the Lord.

"M   A   S

> " His cautious soul's his triumph,
> In Christ is his joy and calling,
> In the heavens his soul liveth,
> His corps till Christ return remaining."

In the churchyard adjoining the abbey there are many old stones, but the inscriptions are much worn, and some of them quite illegible.

On a very small, plain stone :—

"Heir lyes Jams Waker sone to the desisd John Waker who died the 13 of October 1713 and his age . . ."

On a small, curiously-shaped stone :—

"Her lyes Androv Haig who dayed the 20 day Sepm 1679."

On a small, thin stone :—

"Heir lyes Jams Heag son to the descised Willeam Heag . y^s . J . H . was porchioner in Kedslie . A . G . . . who died the 8 of Janw MDCCXIV and of his . . ."

On the other side of this stone are rudely sculptured an uncouth figure, hour-glass, cross bones, and skull.

On a stone erected to the memory of a son of old "Jamie Barrie," who was custodian of the Wallace monument near by, is the following inscription written by himself :—

> "Beneath this stone lies James Barrie,
>   Whose Bible lov'd to read,
> But now in silent tomb does lie,
>   No farther can proceed."

The termination of the above was considered too abrupt, and the following was added :—

> "Until last trumpet's awful sound
>   The rending earth shall shake,
> And opening graves shall yield their dust,
>   And death to life awake.
>   "Aged 25."

The following is a list of the ministers that have been in Mertoun since 1576 :—

> Robert Ker—1576 to 1579.
> Robert Rind—1580 to 1581
> James Menzies—1585 to ——.
> James Smythe, M.A.—1586 to 1592.

John Hepburne, M.A.—1593 to 1596.
Alexander Symsone, M.A.—1597 to 1632.*
James Urquhart, M.A.—1632 to 1635.
Thomas Courtney, M.A.—1640 to ——.
James Kirkton, M.A.—1657 to 1662.
Thomas Courtney, M.A. (reinstated)—1663 to ——.
James Dunbar, M.A.—1667 to 1675.
Andrew Meldrum, M.A.—1675 to 1690.
James Kirkton, M.A. (reinstated)—1690 (a few months).
John Wallace, M.A.—1692 to 1693.
Robert Liver, M.A.—1697 to 1717.
James Innes, M.A.—1718 to 1767.
John Martin—1768 to 1790.
James Duncan—1790 to 1845.
John Grieve—1845 to 1860.
William M'Lean—1860 to 1864.
Alexander M'Laren—1864 to 1891.
Andrew Thomson Donald (present incumbent)—1892.

---

* Symsone, when preaching in Edinburgh, 22d July, 1621, "spared neither king, bishope, nor minister, and found fault with the watchmen of both countries for not admonishing the king to forfeare his oathes, and omitting to put him in mind of the breache of Covenant," for which he was apprehended the following day, and confined to Dumbarton, and ordained to live at his own expense. He was soon again released, and confined to his own parish. "He knew and cared little about earthly things, but was unwearied in prayer, and constantly occupied with the Bible. He died 17th June, 1639."—Scott's *Fasti Ecclesiæ Scoticanæ*.

Mordington.

MENTION is made of the church of Mordington in the year 1275. John de Paxton, who was then parson of the church, was one of the few Scottish ecclesiastics who, at the ecclesiastic council held at Perth in 1275, by order of Pope Gregory X., refused to contribute the tithe of his benefice towards expelling the Saracens from the Holy Land. His successor, Bernard de Lynton, swore fealty to Edward I. on 24th August, 1296.

The ancient church of Mordington stood in a field called the Kirk Park in front of the present mansion house of Mordington. It is said that about the middle of last century it was intentionally set fire to, and completely wrecked. Of that church there are now no remains, but in the centre of the churchyard, near where the old church presumably stood, there is a gloomy old burial vault, which is still very entire. On one side of the doorway facing eastward is the date 1662, with the initial letters W. M. above a heart transfixed with a dagger. The early proprietors of Mordington were members of the Douglas family, which sufficiently explains the above, the armorial bearings referred to being, in part, those used by that powerful family. The letters W. M. probably stand for William Lord Mordington. In the interior there is nothing to relieve the dull monotony of bare walls and a rough, uneven, earthen floor except one curious stone, which is built into the western gable. On this stone or tablet is represented a figure of our Saviour extended upon the cross, with an inscription in rude characters which resemble Hebrew, but which has puzzled the most learned antiquaries to decipher. At its base stand two grotesque and rudely-executed figures, whose heads come immediately below the horizontal cross beam. These figures are attired in a monkish habit. The head of one is surmounted with the *fleur de lis*, and that of the other with the thistle.

The old churchyard, which is now, and has been for many years, in disuse, is in the form of an oval plantation. surrounded with a stone wall which rises about four feet above the general level of the ground outside, and quite level with the inner surface of the burial ground. There are only about a dozen stones to be seen, with fragments of others lying about the surface. A considerable number of other stones, which seem to be almost entire, are level with the ground, and some almost buried out of sight. The whole place, indeed, is in a most dilapidated condition.

A very small stone is thus inscribed :—

"Heir lyes William Ross 1683."

The following appears on a very small, plain stone :—

"Here lays the body of George Spevin who died March 22 day 1745 his age 60 years. Also here lays the body of Allison Broun wife to Georg Spevin who died October 28 day 1735 her age 48 years."

A plain stone is inscribed on one side thus :—

"Here Lyes The Body of Peter Brediy who Died Iune 25 1759 aged 47 years."

On the other side, inscribed within a neat panel, are these words :—

"Here Lyeth The Body of William Brody son to Peter Brody who Died suptember ye 22 day 1752 his age 24 years."

A small and exceedingly plain stone, moss-covered and severely weathered, bears these words :—

"Heir lyes the body of James Cowen who departed this life agvst 27 1733 his age 77 years. And Elizabeth Fish his wife who died in the 8 day of Swptember Anno 1719 aged 56 years."

A church, which was the successor of the original one already referred to, and the predecessor of the present church yet to be noticed, stood in the centre of the present burial ground of Mordington parish, close to the Duns road, four miles from Berwick. This building was used as the parish church up till the time that the present church was erected. There are no traces whatever of this building now, but it is understood to have been a very plain and uninteresting fabric, erected some time during the 17th century.

The churchyard presently in use contains nothing remarkable in the way of old inscriptions, and nothing more remote than the middle of the 18th century.

On a large stone, erected to the memory of Andrew and William Ker, are these words :—

> " Though in the grave my body ly
>   And worms do it consume
> Till waiting for the glorious day
>   When Christ shall call me home.
> Though for a time my dust be loath
>   Most beautiful ill be
> My mortal body shall be cloth'd
>   With immortality."

The following words appear on a medium-sized stone :—

" Heare Lyeth the Body of Jas Hogg ·.· who Died the 26th of Janry 1797 aged 67 years."

A large horizontal stone, with date 1775, has the following lines :—

> " He was healthful
>   And his conscience clear
> His heart was honest
>   To his friends sincere
> Death nere did awe him
>   For he wished to die
> In silent Peace
>   Here let his ashes lie."

The present little church of Mordington is quite modern, having been erected about 25 years ago. It occupies a delightful situation, midway between the old churchyard and the one presently in use, about a quarter of a mile from each. Standing on a high ridge, it commands an extensive view of a far-reaching and beautiful landscape. It is in the Gothic style, and cruciform in shape. The interior is neat, well lighted, lofty, and exceedingly comfortable.

LAMBERTON, which was formerly a parish, is now united to Mordington. Its church was a chapelry belonging to the priory of Coldingham, to which its advowson was attached. After the Reformation Lamberton parish was annexed to the adjoining parish of Ayton to enlarge the stipend; and in 1650 it was disjoined from Ayton and annexed to the still smaller parish of Mordington. The old church of Lamberton stood on an eminence three miles northward from Berwick near the Edinburgh road. It was the scene of several important events. The marriage treaty of Princess Margaret with James IV. stipulated that she should be delivered to the King's commissioners at Lamberton church, without any expense to the bridegroom. The story of her journey hence from Berwick is thus quaintly told:—" On the xxx and xxxi days of July 1502, the queen tarried at Barrwyk, where she had great chere of the said cappitayne of Barrwyk. That same day was, by the cappitayne, to the pleaseur of the said quene, gyffen corses of chasee, within the said town, with other sports of bayrs and of dogs togeder. The first day of August, the quene departed from Barwick for to go to Lamberton kerke in verrey fair company, and well appoynted. Before the said quene war, by order, Johannes and hys company [of players] and Henry Glescebery and his company, the trumpets, officrs of arms, and sergeants of Masse; so that, at the departing out of the said Barrwyk, and at her Bedward, at Lamberton kerke, it was a joy for to see and here."*

Queen Margaret lost her husband at the fatal battle of Flodden in 1513, and in 1517, under sadly

---

* Leland's *Collectanea, II.*

altered circumstances, she returned to Lamberton kirk a widowed queen. The ruins of this church stand within its burying ground, close to the farm steading of the same name. It has consisted of a nave, 30 feet by 17 feet, and a narrower chancel, 28 feet by 14 feet internally, each of which is now converted into a burial-aisle. The walls are about six feet high, and the greater part of these is modern, every detail of ancient date having disappeared.*

The churchyard, which is now in disuse, is in a sadly dilapidated condition, many of the tombstones lying flat on the ground and partially overgrown with grass. The wall which surrounds it is partly broken down, and affords but meagre protection to the sacred place.

On a medium-sized stone, dated 1772, are these words :—

"Vain world, farewell, enough I've had of thee,
For now I'm careless what thou say'st of me :
Thy smiles I court not nor thy frowns do fear,
My cares are past, my bones lie quiet here,
My crimes conspicuous, vain man, avoid !
Thine own heart search and then thou'lt be employed."

---

* Mr Ferguson.—*Hist. Ber. Nat. Club*, 1890.

Several authorities state that the marriage ceremony of James IV. and Margaret was performed in Lamberton church, and a tradition has long prevailed in this part of the country that on this account the King of Scotland granted to the clergyman of this parish and his successors, in all time coming, the liberty of *marrying people without proclamation of banns.* James IV. was not married here, and the tradition referred to has no historical foundation. Lamberton Toll, near by, was long notorious for its irregular marriages, and indeed several have taken place within the last few years. This may have had something to do with the above tradition.

The following appears on a very small stone :—

"Here Lyeth the corps of David Windrham, sons of George Windrham who departed this life March 26, 1767."

A medium-sized, plain stone, dated 1772, is thus inscribed :—

> "Here lyes John Runciman
> Kept within
> A prison close for
> Adam's sin. But rests in
> Glorious hope that he
> Shal by the second
> Adam be set free."

The following is a list of the ministers who have been in Mordington since 1573 :—

Robert Douglas—1573 to 1581.
John Spottiswood—1581 to ——.
Thomas Ramsay, M.A.—1648 to 1682.
George Barclay—1682 to 1689.
Thomas Ramsay, M.A. (reinstated)—1689 to 1695.
Alexander Lauder, M.A.—1695 to 1719.
John Law—1721 to 1735.
Richard Bell, M.A.—1736 to 1773.
James Smith—1773 to 1791.
George Drummond—1792 to 1800.
William Davidson—1801 to 1804.
George Chalmers—1805 to 1831.
George Fulton Knight, M.A.*—1832 to 1843.
Charles Blair—1843 to 1870.
David Miller, B.D., LL.B.—1871 to 1884.
Hugh Fleming (present incumbent)—1885.

There is a Free Church in this parish, built in 1843. The present minister is Peter Geddes Hendry, M.A., settled in 1894.

---

* Knight left the Established Church at the Disruption.

Nenthorn.

The church of Naithansthirn, now Nenthorn, existed in the latter part of the 12th century. Nenthorn and Newton, or Little Newton, were at this time included in the district now embraced in the present parish. Both were originally chapels dependent on the church of Ednam as the mother church, which was a dependency of Coldingham till 1316, when, with its subordinate chapels, it came into the possession of the monks of Kelso, with whom it remained till the Reformation.* In the latter part of the 12th century Nenthorn and Newton were formed into a separate parish, and the chapel of the former became the parish church.

The foundations of the ancient church of Nenthorn are dimly traceable in the centre of the churchyard. A few fragments of sculptured stones, all that have been rescued from the old building, are gathered together in a small heap.

In the churchyard, which occupies a delightfully secluded position on the north bank of the river Eden, are a number of old and interesting stones.

On a medium-sized stone, the upper part of which

---

* Chalmers' *Caledonia*.

is broken away so that the first line of the inscription is awanting, appears the following:—*

"My saul in Hevin
My bones in Hopheir
lyes to rest to reign
in thair Redemer
ryse for satan sin
the grave death
hel and al my savi
our Chryst upon the
croce maid thral.
M B"

the 24 of Apryl 1614.

ounfield good vyf of

sneip qd dyed in Cryst

The following inscription is from a flat tombstone discovered by Mr. C. B. Balfour of Newton Don, who had it cleaned from its centuries' overgrowth of moss and weeds, and copied the words. The Alexander Stevisone mentioned is understood to be an ancestor of Mr. J. H. Rutherfurd, publisher, Kelso.

"HEIR LYIS OF
GVD MEMOR
IE ANE VERIE
HONEST
MAN CALIT
ALEXANDER
STEVISONE
QVHO DE
PARTED YE
S DAY OF
IANUAR YE
ZEIR OF GOD
1606
HE YAT BE
LYVEIS IN
ME SAL
HAVE EV
ERLAST
ING LIFE."

---

* When the author came upon this stone it stood inverted,

Another reads :—

"Heir lyes an honest man James Persone who decaesed May 21 Age 70 1681.

"Heir lyes Margaret daughter to John Pearsone present tenent in Hardis mile place who died the 8 of October 1688 age 17."

On a very small, plain stone :—

"Heir lyes Jenet Stevenson spous to Wiliam Thinn who deceased Novr 22 1695 age 77."

On a very small, sculptured stone :—

"Heir . lyes . William . Watson . Robert . Watson . Jeanet . Watson . children . to . Robert . Watson . died . in . April . 1684."

And on the other side of this stone :—

"Heir . lyes . Elspth . Brovn . died . in Agvst . 1688 . and . Mark . ker . Spovs . to . Robrt . Watson . N . Maxwhilhewgh . dyster . who . died . Agwst . 15 . day . 1702 . year . hir . age . 50."

On a small stone with some grotesquely sculptured figures on it :—

"Death is not loss but rather gain
If we by dying life a tine."

A similar stone bears :—

"Heir lyes Thomas Whit merchant who died Agust 2 1687 and of his age 85 years."

---

so that the upper part of the inscription was buried more than a foot below the surface of the ground. For the correct rendering of this and other inscriptions which follow, he is indebted to Mr. Balfour, who, referring to the letters "M B," observes :— "The initials 'M B' perhaps show that Mary or Margaret Brounfield was the name. Sneip is a cottage on Mellerstain estate, close to Mellowlees."

The present church is small and quite modern, having been erected in 1802. It is situated about a quarter of a mile from the site of the old church and burial-ground.

There are two communion cups, engraved

"NENTHORN PARISH 1780."

Of the CHAPEL of NEWTON there is not a vestige now remaining; even its exact site is a matter of uncertainty. Referring to it, Mr. Balfour says:—
"This chapel has a long history. The chapels of Little Newton, Nathansthyrne, and Stitchell were originally chapels of the mother church of Ednam. In 1158–63 they belonged to Coldingham Priory, a dependency of Durham. In 1204 the monks conceded to William, Bishop of St. Andrews, both chapels of Newton and Nathanshorn. David of Bernham, Bishop of St. Andrews (1238–52), is said to have consecrated the church of Nenthorn, which probably then became the parish church, and the chapel of Little Newton the dependent chapel, instead of both being chapels of Ednam. In 1316 William of Lamberton, Bishop of St. Andrews, gave the church of Nenthorn and the chapel of Little Newton to the Abbey of Kelso, in exchange for Cranston and Preston in Mid-Lothian. In 1567 the 'kirklands of Nenthorne' are entered as producing a rental of forty shillings, and the 'lands of Lytill Nutowne' thirty shillings.

"The site of the chapel of Little Newton is probably the old burial-place of the Don family, outside the Mid-Lodge of Newton Don. The only other possible site is in the Lawn Park, where the site of the village is said to have been. Here, when laying drains some years ago, the workmen came on stone coffins, which were left *in situ*."*

The walls of the burial vault referred to above, which seems to be comparatively modern, are still standing. The place is not now used as the family burying vault. Lying just outside the walls is a fragment of an old tombstone, with a part of the inscription, thus:—

". . . . .
"and Margt. Novr 14 1729 years."

Near it is a fragment of another apparently much older stone, with grotesque figure in relief sculptured upon it, but without any inscription.

The following is a list of the ministers that have been in Nenthorn since 1597:—

    John Spottiswood—1597 to 1611.
    Andrew Kinneir, M.A.—1611 to ——.
    James Fletcher, M.A.—1660 to 1662.
    James Robesone—1664 to ——.
    James Fletcher, M.A. (reinstated)—1669 to ——.
    Robert Calder—1689 to 1689 (a few months).
    William Brown, M.A.—1692 to 1692 (a few months).
    James Ker, M.A.—1696 to 1754.
    Abraham Ker—1754 to 1793.
    Gavin Wallace—1793 to 1834.
    John Gifford (assistant and successor)—1832 to 1854.
    Manners H. Graham—1855 to 1866.
    John Barclay—1866 to 1868.
    Henry G. Graham—1868 to 1884.
    David Anderson (present incumbent)—1885.

---

* Paper by C. B. Balfour, Esq., Newton Don.—*Hist. Ber. Nat. Club.*

There is a Free Church in this parish, built in 1843. It is in the Gothic style; small, but very comfortable. The present minister is Donald Iverach, M.A., settled in 1885.

Polwarth.

So far as the mere fabric is concerned, there are few churches in Berwickshire more interesting than that of Polwarth. Its position on an elevation, embowered in wood and clothed in a lovely green mantle of ivy, is exceedingly picturesque. It is situated almost in the very heart of Berwickshire, midway between Duns and Greenlaw.

The following inscription appears on a sandstone slab inserted in the wall above the south door:—

" Templum · hoc · dei · cultui · in · ecclesia · de · Poluarth ·
   A · fundi · dominis · ejusdem · prius · designationis ·
Dein · cognominis · ædificatum · et · dicatum · ante · annum ·
   Solutis · 900 · rectoriaque · beneficio · dotatum ·
     sed · temporis · cursu · labefactum ·
A · dno · Johanne · de · sancto · claro · de · Herdmanston ·
   Genero · dni · patricij · de · Poluarth · de · eodem ·
     circa · annum · 1378 · reparatum ·
Tandem · vero · vetustate · ad · ruinam · vergens ·
   Sumtibus · utriusque · prosaplæ · heredis ·
Dni · patricij · Hume · comitis · de · Marchmont · etc ·
   summi · scotiæ · cancellarii ·
Et · dnæ · Griselliæ · Kar · comitissæ · suæ · sposæ ·
Sepulchri · sacello · arcuate · reçens · constructum ·
   Et · campanarum · obelisco · adauctum · fuit ·
     Anno · domini · 1703."*

---

* Translation :—" This temple for the worship of God in the church of Polwarth by the lords of the soil of the same designation originally, afterwards of the same name, built and consecrated before the year of grace 900, and endowed with the

On 7th April, 1242, the church was dedicated (re-dedicated, we should say, according to the theory of its antiquity as stated in the inscription) by Bishop David de Bernham. In 1296 Adam Lamb, the "parson of the church of Paulesworth," swore fealty to Edward I., and, in consequence, had his forfeited property restored. He continued in office till 1299, when Edward presented William de Sandyntone, clerk, to the living. In 1378 the church—not, we may presume, a very durable or imposing edifice—had fallen into a ruinous state, and was then repaired by Lord John Sinclair of Herdmanston.

---

benefice of a rector, but in course of time fallen into ruin, was repaired by Lord John Sinclair of Herdmanston, the son-in-law of Lord Patrick Hume, Earl of Marchmont, &c., High Chancellor of Scotland, and of Lady Grissoll Kar, his wife and countess, it was fresh built with the shrine in the form of a vault, and augmented by the addition of a bell-tower. Anno Domini 1703."

From this it would appear that Polwarth can boast of a higher antiquity than any others (save the priory churches) in Berwickshire. It is unfortunate, however, that the evidence is barely sufficient to warrant our acceptance of so remote an antiquity as that which the foregoing inscription ascribes to it. On this point Mr Ferguson remarks :—" The statement in the Latin inscription that it was endowed as a rectory before the year 900 does not appear to be supported by sufficient evidence, although the old spelling of the name Paulworth points to a Saxon origin."

On the other hand, Miss Warrender (herself a descendant of the Homes of Polwarth, and able therefore to speak with authority), in her admirable and carefully-written work, *Marchmont and the Homes of Polwarth*, seems to have no doubts as to the antiquity of this church. She says :—" Ten centuries have passed since the pious zeal of those far distant days dedicated a church here to St. Mungo, the 'Beloved Saint,' the memory of whose miracles and blameless life was still fresh in the land."

Adam Hume, third son of Sir Patrick, the fourth Baron of Polwarth, was rector of the church at the time of the Reformation.

The armorial bearings of the Hume family adorn the tower, while the crowned orange (Marchmont arms) surmounts the eastern gable.

The Marchmont family proved liberal benefactors in the repairing and furnishing the church. For the new tower, which was erected in 1703, a handsome bell was given by Lady Marchmont, and inscribed thus:—

"Given to the Kirk of Polwarth by Lady Grizel Kar Countess of Marchmont, 1697. R.M. Fecit Edr. 1717."

This benefactress seems to have gifted the bell twenty years before it was made.

There is a quaint, old-fashioned look about the building which lends a peculiar charm to a place already hallowed by associations that have made Polwarth to be ever memorable in other than a merely ecclesiastical sense. The old vault beneath the church is that in which Sir Patrick Hume lay concealed for over a month. He suffered thus on account of his religious convictions. His wife, Lady Polwarth, and his daughter Grisell, then a girl of eighteen, alone knew where he was hidden. With the aid of another, the house carpenter, whom they admitted into their confidence, they conveyed into the vault during night a bed and bedclothes. The bed is still preserved at Marchmont, and bears the date 1860.* To-day as then

---

* The story of Sir Patrick's experiences is thus graphically

the vault is lit by a faint glimmering light from the grating high up in the eastern end, through which those outside, by stooping down on the grass, may distinguish—when their eyes become accustomed to the dusky gloom—four coffins, once richly gilt

---

told by a descendant of his own:—"For a month (so Lady Murray, Lady Grisell Baillie's daughter, relates in her *Memoirs*, from which most of these particulars are gathered) Sir Patrick lived in this dismal hiding-place. The only light that reached him was through the narrow slit at the end of the vault, as it was too great a risk to have any artificial light inside. Reading was impossible; but he got through the long hours by repeating to himself Buchanan's version of the Psalms, which he knew by heart, and which he remembered to his dying day. Every night his daughter Grisell came by stealth, carrying him food and drink, and enlivening his solitude with the home news, stories of his children, their sayings and doings, and anything she could think of to cheer and amuse him. The first glimmerings of dawn sent her hurrying homewards, fearful of being surprised by one of the parties of soldiers that were scouring the country in search of her father. Her dread of this overcame her natural fear of crossing the churchyard after dark. The first night that she went there she was terrified by the barking of the minister's dogs (the manse then stood much nearer the church than it does now), and feared they might give the alarm; but her mother next morning sent for the minister, and, under pretence of a mad dog being loose in the country, induced him to destroy them. The little lantern that she carried still exists, of very rude make, three-sided, and with hinges of roughly-tanned cow-hide. For fear of exciting the suspicions of the servants, she had to convey part of her own dinner off her plate into her lap, in order to secure food for her father; and it was on one of these occasions that her little brother Sandy (afterwards the second Lord Marchmont) turned to Lady Polwarth in consternation and complained, 'Mother, will ye look at Grisell? while we have been eating our broth, she has eaten up the whole sheep's head!' When Sir Patrick heard of this he was greatly amused, and desired that Sandy should have his share next time."— *Marchmont and the Humes of Polwarth.*

and decorated, now with tarnished plates and nails, and mouldering velvet palls.*

Above the two old doorways on the front wall of the church are engraved verses taken from the Bible. On the south-east wall is an inscription in memory of Adam Hume, the first Protestant minister (1567 to 1593). There are two other memorial stones built into the outer wall, also in memory of former ministers: one to Alexander Cass, who died in the year 1651, the other to George Holiwell, who is quaintly described as "pedagogue" to Patrick, Earl of Marchmont, and whose father was a periwig-maker in Duns, died 1704.

In old days a bell used to be carried in the funeral processions at Polwarth, and rung in front of the coffin to frighten away the evil spirits. The bell still exists, but is at present in possession of the family of the late minister. A good many years ago, the basin of the old font was discovered hidden away at the back of the church. It is now placed on a graduated circular base on the grass close to the west door, and is a rude, circular, sandstone basin without carving or ornament of any kind, and apparently of early date. The external diameter is 28 inches, and the height $20\frac{1}{2}$ inches, the depth of the bowl being 14 inches, with a perforation at the bottom.†

The interior of the church is, like the exterior, exceedingly quaint and old-fashioned, and bears

---

* *Marchmont and the Humes of Polwarth.*
† *Marchmont and the Humes of Polwarth.*

the marks of antiquity on the walls and roof. The old hangings which still adorn the pulpit—now covered over with a cloth of more modern and less artistic kind—were embroidered in a most elaborate arabasque pattern by Lady Grisell Baillie. On one of the walls is a marble slab, which records that Hugh, Earl of Marchmont, raised this monument to the eternal memory of the most obedient and incomparable of wives. The inscription, which is in Latin, runs thus:—

> "MEMORIÆ ÆTERNÆ
> ANNÆ WESTERN,
> HUGO COMES DE MARCHMONT,
> CONJUGI INCOMPARABILI
> OBSEQUENTISSIMÆ
> ET OPLIMÆ DE SE MERITÆ
> POSUIT
> EJUSQUE CORPUS IN ARCA
> HIC CONDIDIT."

The communion plate consists of two silver cups, engraved:—

"These cups are given to the kirk of Poluarth by Lady Jean Hume, Lady Poluarth."

The churchyard surrounds the church, and contains some very old stones; but many of these have their inscriptions so weathered and effaced as to be quite illegible.

The following lines appear on a large stone:—

> " Beneath this stone the hand of death fast binds
> A form once active learned generous and kind
> Whose liberal soul to all men did extend
> A friend to all : all men to him a friend."

On a small stone are these words :—

"Margret Milton spows to Thomas Stevnson who dyod janwary the 12 1696 her age . . ."

The following appears on a very small, curiously shaped stone :—

"1699
Remember man as thou gost by
As thou art nou so once was I
As I am nou so most ye be
Remember man tht ye most die."

A small stone is inscribed thus :—

"Here leys Margret Wait daughter to James Wait who died y 4th of Oct 1734 & in the 27 of her age."

Another small stone, with ornamental margin, and bearing a cherub on the top, has these words on one side :—

"Here lyes Jean Greig Spouse to Patrick Christie who died in June 1690."

On the other side :—

"P C   I G
Memento Mori."

Another very small stone is thus inscribed :—

"Hir lyeth cris Tier Ridpath who died 1710 29 of Septembr"

The following is a list of the ministers of Polwarth since 1567 :—

Adam Hume—1567 to 1593.
Alexander Gaittis, M.A.—1593 to 1603.
Alexander Cass or Case, M.A.*—1604 to 1651
David Robertson, M.A.—1652 to 1663.
George Holiwell, M.A.—1664 to 1704.
Archibald Borthuik, M.A.—1709 to 1727.
John Hume—1727 to 1734.
William Home—1735 to 1758.
Alexander Hume—1758 to 1768.
Robert Home—1768 to 1838.
Walter Home (assis. and succ.)—1823 to 1881.
Charles James Watt, M.A. (present incumbent)—1882.

---

* Cass was a member of the General Assembly in 1638, and being first in the roll gave his vote with some pleasant or witty remark on the grave and solemn questions which occupied their deliberations, for which he was thus lampooned at the time:—

> "From the most stupid senseles asse,
> That ever brayed, my cousin Casse;
> He is the Assembly's voyce, and so
> The Assembly is his echo.
> The fool speaks first, and all the rest
> To say the same are ready prest."
> —Scott's *Fasti Ecclesiæ Scoticanæ*.

Swinton.

The church of Swinton is very ancient. The present parish of that name is composed of the two previously independent parishes of Swinton and Simprin. These were united in 1761, when the latter ceased to exist. In the year 1098, when Coldingham was founded, King Edgar dedicated the church of Swinton, and consigned to the monks of that monastery upon the altar "Villam totam Swinton cum divisis, sicut Liulf habuit." This grant of Edgar was confirmed by his successor and by Bishop Robert in 1150, in presence of his Synod at Berwick. The church remained in the possession of Coldingham till the Reformation.

In 1296 William de Swinton, the vicar of Swinton, swore fealty to Edward I. at Berwick.

William Bartrem, a person of some note, was "Vicar of Swynton" in 1455, and received considerable possessions from the then proprietor, John of Swinton.*

---

* The deed of acknowledgment from the vicar's hand is an interesting document, dated 16th June, 1455, and runs thus :—

"Till all and sindry qwhais knawlage thir present lettres sal cum, Wilzem Bartrem, perpetuale wicare of the parroche kyrk of Swynton, gretyng in God aylestande : Yhoure vniuersite mot wit that the xvj day of the moneth of Junij, the zher of God a thousand foure hundredth fifty and fywe zheris, in the presens of honorable men, that is to say, Alexander of Cockburn of Langtoun, Adam of Nesbit of that ilke, Robert of Blakater of that

The original edifice was replaced in 1593 by a rude building similar in style to those which prevailed during that period. Considerable portions of this building, the foundations included, still remain, although the greater part was replaced by another in 1792. The old fabric (the building of 1593) was taken down on account of an apprehension that it was in a ruinous and dangerous state, whereas, on setting about pulling it down, it appeared to be uncommonly strong, and might have stood for ages.*

An old stone, built into the east gable of the church, bears the Swinton arms, with initials and date, thus :—

```
      " S
    A     S
    M     H
    16    35,"
```

ilke, Thomas Dyksoun of Marsyntoun and Jhon Dyksoun his brother, and diuerse vtheris, at the request and counsale of thaime, an honorable man, Jhon of Swinton of that ilke, gafe to me for all the dayis and tym of my life, all and hale his medow lande, lyande betuix the fwrsene lande pertenyng to me be resoun of the kirk lande of the said wicarage, ande the water of Lete fra the estende of my sade fursen lande, lyand of southhalf the water of Lete, to the westend of the fursen lande of the samyn, for myn orgsoun alanerly, dayly to be maid for all the dayis of my life, for the saide Jhon of Swyntoun of that ilke, his wif, his barnys, thare antecessouris; the quhilk medow he promittit and sufferit me till occupy be wertu of his gift of the samyn to me for my liftyme, for myn orisoun to be maid dayly as said is, and be nane other resoun : and this till all and sindry to qwham it afferis or may affere in tyme to cum I mak it knawyn be thir present lettres : In witnes of the qwhilk thing I have hunge to my seil at Swyntoun, day of the moneth and yhere before wrytyn."—*The Swintons of that Ilk and their Cadets.*

* *Old Statistical Account.* Mr. Ferguson having carefully examined the building, is of opinion that the lower portions of the east, south, and west walls are original.

signifying Sir Alexander Swinton and (dame) Margaret Home. A mural tablet on the north wall, with a similar device, but more rudely carved, may be supposed to mark their graves. The following dates appear above the east and west windows respectively:—"A.D. 1796; A.D. 1800." These doubtless refer to minor additions and repairs.

In 1782 a handsome aisle was built to the north side. This was executed at the expense of "a party of the fewars of Swinton," and in a great measure at their own expense. It is called "The Feurs' Aisle," and on the interior wall is inscribed the names of the "party" referred to, numbering 18.

Many generations of the ancient Swinton family lie buried within the walls of the church. A stone figure of Sir Alan de Swinton, the fifth baron of that family, lies in an arched open niche on the south wall to the right of the pulpit: under rudely-sculptured figures of a boar and three boars' heads (the proper charges of the family, though here singularly marshalled) is the inscription:—

"Hic . Iacet . Alanvs . Svintonvs . Miles . de . eodem."

Below is a full-length figure of the knight, with his arms bent upwards from the elbows, and clasping what resembles a book. There is no date, but it is well known that this Sir Alan died about the year 1200. Some authorities maintain that what he holds in his hands is a stone, and that, by immemorial tradition, this is said to allude to a large clue of yarn, by the dexterous use of which in one hand, while he used his sword with the other, he dispatched a great wild boar in that field in Swinton

Hill which, from that event, still retains the name of "Allan's Cairn."* A vault in front of the monument, and under the floor of the church, having been opened some years ago, was found to contain a coffin and three skulls; one of these, which was of unusual dimensions, was supposed to be that of Sir Alan.

The bell is old, and bears this inscription:—

"MARIA EST NOMEN MEVM."

Following this are four peculiarly-shaped characters, which were probably originally intended to represent a date. They have been submitted to a London expert to decipher, but without success.

The churchyard contains nothing very remarkable, the inscriptions on the older stones being quite illegible.

These words are inscribed on the bevelled edges of a large horizontal stone:—

"Here lyes Will Veatch son to Mr. Hen Veatch and Martha Gardiner who died Maye the 12 1726 His age 1 year."

SIMPRIN.—This church existed in the time of David I. (1124–1153), when "Hye de Simpring" possessed the manor of Simprin and the advowson of its church. The same proprietor, during Malcolm IV.'s reign (1153–1165), granted to the monks of Kelso the church of Simprin, with a toft and some lands.† It was dedicated by Bishop Bernham in 1247.

---

* *The Swintons of that Ilk and their Cadets. Old Statistical Account.*
† Chalmers'.*Caledonia.*

Simprin church is honourably associated with the name of Thomas Boston, author of *The Four-fold State:* a man of deep piety and superlative zeal in the cause of religion. He was minister of Simprin between 1699 and 1707.

In 1761 Simprin ceased to be a separate parish, and was then annexed to Swinton. After this the church was allowed to go to ruin.

It has been a very small building, consisting of a nave and chancel, the former 22 feet long by 13 feet wide, and the latter 23 feet long by 16 feet wide. The east gable is still almost entire; the north wall of the chancel remains, to the height of about 6 feet; but all the other portions are nearly level with the ground. The only window now visible is a small round-headed one, in the centre of the east gable, measuring 2 feet 9 inches by 1 foot 3 inches, bevelled outside, and widely splayed laterally, but flat-headed, within. There seem to have been two doorways, opening into the nave and chancel respectively, through the south wall; and one of the stones of the east jamb of the chancel doorway, broadly chamfered on the outer edge, may still be seen. With such vague and imperfect details, it is impossible to pronounce with confidence upon the age of the building, but it can hardly be later than the thirteenth century.[*]

The ruins, in the middle of the now-disused burial-ground, stand in a small plantation about a mile and a half to the east of Swinton. The place is in a sadly dilapidated condition, and the stones,

---

[*] Mr. Ferguson.—*Hist. Ber. Nat. Club,* 1890.

about a score or more in number, are lying about in a disorderly and uncared-for fashion—a discredit to the community, and especially to those who are mainly responsible for such a state of things.

There are several old and very interesting stones in the churchyard.

A small, neatly-carved stone bears these words:—

"1610.
"Heir lyes under this ston the body of Willeam Cockbourn whos dayes was feu. his glass it was soon run. all that him knew their lov he wan who departed July 28."

On another small stone :—

"Heiar layes the body of Magret Common who departed this lyfe the 19 day Iwlay 1719 hir age was 60."

The following appears on a large horizontal stone, and refers to James Gibson, one of the ministers of Simprin :—

"Hic jacet Mr Jacobus Gibson pernuper sacerdos ecclesiae Simprinensis qui obiit 2º Martii Anno Domini 1668."

The following is a list of the ministers that have been in Swinton since 1590 :—

> Robert Hislop—1590 to 1595.
> Andrew Arbuthnot—1595 to 1632.
> Walter Swintoun, M.A.—1632 to 1646.
> Edward Jameson, M.A.*—1647 to 1661.
> Patrick Suintoune, M.A.—1668 to 1685.
> Edward Jameson, M.A. (reinstated)—1687 to 1691.
> Robert Sandelands—1691 to 1695.
> John Lithgow—1695 to 1711.
> Henry Veatch, M.A.—1712 to 1753.

---

* A decree was passed against Jameson in 1671 for preaching at Conventicles, on which he was outlawed in 1676.

George Cupples—1754 to 1798.
William Simson—1799 to 1804.
James Baird—1804 to 1814.
John Hunter—1814 to 1832.
James Logan—1833 to 1868.
Robert Home—1868 to 1877.
Alexander Milne—1878 to 1884.
James Gordon—1884 to 1891.
D. D. F. Macdonald (present incumbent)—1892.

SIMPRIN.

Thomas Boner, M.A.—1606 to 1632.
John Markmath, M.A.—1632 to 1638.
Robert Meluill—1641 to 1654.
James Gibson—1668 to 1668 (a few months).
James Sanderson, M.A.—1668 to 1671.
George Wilsone—1672 to 1683.
James Adamson—1689 to 1689 (a few months).
John Moir—1691 to ——.
Thomas Boston, M.A.—1699 to 1707.
James Allan—1707 to 1716.
James Chrystie, M.A.—1717 to 1725.
James Landereth, M.A.—1725 to 1756.
John Jolly—1757 to 1761.

There is a Free Church at Swinton, erected in 1860 (second since the Disruption). It is a handsome building, with spire, in which there is a clock. It is oblong, 70 feet by 35, Gothic roof and windows; capable of accommodating 520. The present minister is William Shearer, ordained in 1870.

Westruther.

This parish is not ancient, having been formed about the middle of the seventeenth century (1649). Originally, it belonged to the parish of Home, from which, at the Reformation, it was disjoined, and annexed to the parish of Gordon. On account of the distance of the church of Gordon from the Westruther and Bassendean district, a minister was appointed in 1647 to the chapel of Bassendean. With a view to the convenience and better accommodation of the people in the northern part of this parish, a church was built at the village of Westruther in 1649, and it was then constituted a separate and independent parish.

The original church of Westruther, therefore, cannot boast of any great antiquity. It is now disused, and the ruins, which stand in the centre of the burying ground, are rapidly falling to decay. Originally, it was a plain building, covered over with heather without and unceiled within, but much larger and more commodious than it now is. In 1752 it underwent important alterations and repairs, besides being reduced to about one-third its original dimensions. It would seem that this was rendered necessary mainly by the large numbers who went over to the Secessionists at that time. The building, which is almost completely overgrown with ivy, has a picturesque, and even venerable, appearance.

There are several interesting stones in the churchyard.

These words appear on one side of a medium-sized stone :—

"Here lies the remains of the dust of John Wright who died March th 28 1781 aged 27 years."

On the other side :—

"Remember man as you pass by
As you are now so once was I
And as I am so shall you be
Remember man that you must die
But mind with all the day will come
Whereon thy judge will doom
You for the deeds that you have done
He who loves God's abode and to combine
With saints on earth shall one day with them shine."

On a small stone :—

"Here lys Gilbert . . . who died in Re . . cleugh the 27 of December the year 1701."

On a small, very plain stone, in large letters :—

"Hear lyes James Redpath and his children 1 May 1699."

On a small thick stone :—

"1674 G . F . I . Y."

BASSENDEAN.—When the original church of Bassendean was reared we have no means of determining. Probably it never was a place of much ecclesiastical importance, although it was served by a vicar long before the Reformation. It belonged to Coldingham, and was dedicated to the Virgin.

A considerable portion of the old Roman Catholic chapel—used as such prior to the Reformation—is still in existence. Its remains, with those of the churchyard, occupy a grassy knoll three miles to the south of Westruther, and about a mile from the village of Houndslow. It has been a plain rectangular structure, 54½ feet long by about 20 feet wide externally. The walls, which are 3 feet thick, remain to the height of about 11 feet, but both gables are wanting. Outside, the north-east and west walls are without any decorative details; the south wall is pierced by a doorway about 16 feet from its western extremity, and by two square-headed windows in its eastern portion, about 11½ feet apart. The doorway is a plain, bevel-edged opening, 6 feet high by 3 feet 3 inches wide; the windows are more elaborately treated, having widely counter-splayed jambs which present externally a double splay, the outer plain, the inner, which is also the narrower of the two, fluted; and internally a succession of plain and moulded chamfer orders, with an edge-roll flanked by two hollows. The lights have been placed near the centre of the wall. The westermost window is 3½ feet high by 1 foot 8 inches wide, and is of one light only; the other window has been divided into two lights by a monial, now broken away. Judging from the mouldings, the windows seem to have been insertions of Second-Pointed date; and they have evidently been again altered and somewhat contracted in dimensions at a still more recent period, the moulded jambs being partly concealed on the inside by rough masonry.*

It is not possible to ascertain the age of this building. There are several features which point to its being of pre-Reformation date.† In the south wall there is a small rectangular niche or recess, which Mr. Ferguson very properly suggests may have been a receptacle for a holy water-stoup. In other parts of the interior wall there are an ambery and a niche, which the same authority suggests may have contained a piscina. The mutilated remains of the baptismal font lie amongst some loose stones and rubbish. It is a very plain specimen, broken in two pieces, with the usual perforation in the bottom. An old sepulchral slab is utilised to form the lintel of a window, and has sculptured upon it a sword, and a star within a circle. Another similar stone bears a Maltese cross, enclosed in a circle, and a pair of shears below. A plain stone, standing against the interior wall, is inscribed, thus:—

---

* Mr. Ferguson.—*Hist. Ber. Nat. Club*, 1890.

† Dr. Hardy is of opinion that the ruin, as above described, is not a pre-Reformation structure. He describes it as "a mean post-Reformation structure. Before the front door of Bassendean," Dr. Hardy continues, "there is a great sandstone slab, closely resembling others in Gordon churchyard, derived from Greenlaw quarry. This tombstone was removed by a former tenant from Bassendean churchyard. The popular notion is that it commemorates a 'General Leslie,' who fell while fighting against Cromwell. This is unlikely. Most of the other gravestones were used in building farm cottages some years ago. The churchyard is now united to an adjoining grass field."—*Hist. Ber. Nat. Club.*

```
            "D.M.           M.I.D.
             A.D.    B.G.    B.C.
                     1750."
```

Another stone bears

"1763 July."

There is the faint outline of a wall which apparently has enclosed the churchyard. Two or three small fragments are all that now remain, and these are so mutilated that it is with great difficulty we are able at all to discover any evidence of their sacred function.

SPOTTISWOOD lies about two miles south-west of Westruther. Here, during the reign of David II. (1329-1370), John de Spottiswoode built a chapel, called Whitechapel, which was subordinate to the church of Hume.* The ruins of this chapel were entirely swept away when the ground was cleared for building the present offices of Spottiswood, about the beginning of the present century.† The only relic still preserved is the old baptismal font.

At WEDDERLEY, a mile to the north of Westruther, there was formerly a chapel, also subordinate to Home. In the reign of William the Lion (1165-1214) Gilbert, son of Adam of Home, gave to the monks of Kelso the chapel of Wedderley, with ten acres of land, with pasture for sheep and cattle.‡ Of this chapel nothing now remains. A

---

* Chalmers' *Caledonia*.
† *New Statistical Account*.
‡ Chalmers' *Caledonia*. *Chartulary of Kelso*.

ruined vault connected with it was in existence in 1834, and is still remembered by some of the older inhabitants of the district.

The present church of Westruther, which stands within a few yards of the old church already referred to, is quite modern, having been erected about fifty years ago. It is a neat, substantial edifice, presenting, however, no features of special interest.

There is a communion cup belonging to Westruther inscribed :—

"CALIX EUCHARISTICUS ECCLESIÆ PAROCHIALIS WESTRUTHER-ENSIS. A.D. 1718."

The following is a list of the ministers that have been in Westruther since 1574 :—

Ninian Borthwick—1574 to ——.
Thomas Storie—1597 to ——.
John Vetche, M.A.—1648 to 1662.
—— —— —16— to ——.
John Vetche, M.A.* (reinstated)—1680 to 1680 (a few months).
George Wilsone—1683 to 1690.
John Vetche, M.A. (again reinstated)—1690 to 1702.
Walter Scott, M.A.—1704 to 1737.
Francis Scott—1738 to 1781.
William Shiels, M.A.—1782 to 1813.

---

* Vetche was summoned before the Privy Council, 5th Oct., 1680, and, not appearing, was denounced and put to the horn. He was subsequently taken, and kept close prisoner at Edinburgh, under great privations, being neither allowed fire nor candle, nor could his wife have access to speak to him except in presence of witnesses, all on account of his return without a licence. He was deprived for not taking the test. When obliged to leave, he pointed out to his successor a peat stack, requesting him to leave one similar to him should he return again.—Scott's *Fasti Ecclesiæ Scoticanæ*.

John Shiels—1813 to 1819.
John Birrell, M.A.—1819 to 1825.
William Fleming—1826 to 1829.
Robert Jamieson—1830 to 1837.
Walter Wood, M.A.*—1838 to 1843.
Henry Taylor, D.D.—1844 to 1896.
John Muirhead, B.D. (present incumbent)—1896.

The Free Church in this parish is a beautiful and durable edifice, erected in 1854 (being the second church since the Disruption). The present minister is Robert Arthur, M.A., settled in 1888.

---

* Wood was one of those who left the Established Church at the Disruption.

Whitsome.

WHITSOME is made up of the two ancient parishes of Whitsome and Hilton. In 1735 they were united, and the latter ceased to have a separate parochial existence. We are not able to trace the existence of the church of Whitsome further back than 1296, when Rauf de Hawden, parson of the church of Whitsome, along with other "reverend traitors," swore fealty to Edward I. at Berwick. Doubtless it existed considerably prior to this, though it does not appear in the list of churches dedicated by Bishop de Bernham in the middle of the 13th century. Whitsome appears to have been a rectory up till the Reformation.

There are now no remains of the old church of Whitsome, which stood in the centre of the churchyard still in use. The writer of the "Old Statistical Account" (about the latter end of last century) says:—"The church was in my remembrance a miserable thatched building, which, though now slated, is still very ill seated, narrow, and incommodious."

The famous Boston on one occasion officiated in this old church, then thatched; and such a multitude of people flocked from all quarters that many, in their eagerness to hear him, mounted the roof of the humble edifice, tore off portions of the straw, and thus contrived to gratify both eye and ear.

The present church is situated about 200 paces from the churchyard, and was built in 1803. It is small and unpretentious in style, but comfortable inside.

The communion plate consists of two silver cups, engraved :—

"Gifted by A. A. Countes of Home to the Kirk of Whitsome 1704."

They bear also the Home arms.

Some old and very interesting stones appear in the churchyard, which is situated on an elevated position overlooking a fine country, and commanding an extensive view in almost all directions.

On a small plain stone :—

"I   H
1690."

On a long narrow stone :—

"Here lyes the body of Iohn Dickson uho deperted this life the 26 of Nouember 1724 his age 74. Also Margret Loden his spous who Died 1740 aged 70."

On a very small stone :—

"Heire lyeth the corp of Gorg Ald uho left this life 2 of Iun . . . . 93."

(The above date was probably 1693.)

A similar stone bears :—

"HERE LYES ISBEL Dickson spowes to JOHN Shiel who lived in Stowood who died March the 24 1755 aged 60 years."

A large, plain stone, with the figure of a sword rudely carved on its surface, has these initials and dates :—

"W P 1664   G P 1620   G A 1650."

On a large stone with inscription very much defaced :—

"Dauid Innerwick 24 . . . 1618 (?). Here lyeth the corps of William Innerwick son to Georg Innerwick som time portioner of Whitsome who departed this life the 7 day of March in the yeare of God 1628 and of his age the 18 years."

HILTON.—Of this church we have no mention earlier than 1243. It was then dedicated by Bishop de Bernham, and was of old a rectory. In 1296 David, the parson of Hilton, swore fealty to Edward I. at Berwick. In the year 1464 there seems to have been a suit depending at the court of Rome about the church of Hilton.

Only a small fragment of the old church fabric is now standing, which, together with some low mounds, almost entirely overgrown with grass, indicates the position and extent of the building, which has been of the usual long and narrow type. The site is a grassy knowe, close to the farm steading of Hilton, and about a mile to the east of Whitsome.

Hilton bell, which had been rung by the hand, is still preserved. It has inscribed on the rim in legible characters :—" For Hiltoun, 1718."

In the churchyard there are only about a score of tombstones, scattered about promiscuously. Some of these are gradually sinking below the ground, while others are being broken into fragments. The whole place is in a most shameful and neglected condition, utterly unworthy of its sacred office and traditions.

On a small stone are these words:—

"Here lyeth the body of Thomas Purves son to Willeam Purves in Crosrige who died Janr. the 1 1729 His age 17."

A large horizontal stone bears several dates almost illegible, amongst others 1645.

On a very large, plain stone:—

"Here lyes the Body of Mr Daniel Douglas, minister of the Gospel at Hiltoune who departed this life the 24th July anno 1705 his age 86.

"Renewed by Subscription in 1836."

On a very small stone:—

"G. A. 1661   A. G. 1666
A. A. 1664."

On a similar stone:—

"G. M. 1668   . . 1666."

On another small stone:—

"A · M · 1642."

On a medium-sized stone:—

"Heare lays the body of Will Mason who died 3 1771 aged 2 years."

A small stone bears these words:—

"Here lye the corpse of Margrat Clarie who departed xxx of October 1696."

On a similar stone:—

"Heir lyeth James Swine 1677."

P

The following inscription appeared on a stone here, but it is now quite illegible :—

"Heire lyes Christian Forret daughter of James Forret of that Ilk in Fyffe, her mother being daughter to the laird of Lethiday in Angus, married William Somervil of Moshat Girfilman in Clidisdail, with whom she lived a year and being delivered of one daughter, christianly and comfortably past from her pilgrimage to her home and husband Christ Junii 18, 1645.

> What Graces, gifts, parts, perfections rare,
> Among all other women scattered are,
> Unitely, fully, cleirly shined in that star."

The following is a list of the ministers of Hilton from 1585 till the time of its union with Whitsome in 1735 :—

>Andrew Winchester—1585 to 1598.
>James Home—1609 to ——.
>Daniel Douglas, M.A.—1650 to 1662.
>George Hollwell, M.A.—1662 to 1664.
>John Hepburne, M.A.—1664 to 1673.
>William Methven, M.A.—1675 to 1682.
>Simon Wyld—1683 to 1684.
>John Home—1689 to 1690.
>Daniel Douglas, M.A.* (reinstated)—1690 to 1705.

---

* Douglas was minister when the tide of persecution ran high. There is a popular tradition to the effect that one day, during public worship, an individual of the dominant party, offended at certain words which fell from the preacher, laid violent hands upon him, and dragged him from the pulpit. A slight effusion of blood was the consequence, on which the maltreated pastor predicted, in the hearing of the congregation, that the cowardly assailant's blood would yet stain the floor of the sanctuary, and be licked by dogs. It happened soon after that the person from whom Mr. Douglas suffered such ill-usage received a mortal wound from an enemy. A crowd of attendants proceeded homewards with the corpse, but on their way they were overtaken by a storm, which forced them to the nearest

William Wilsone—1707 to 1731.
George Hume—1732 to 1736.

The following is a list of the ministers of Whitsome since 1585.

Thomas Ogilvy—1585 to ——.
Robert Hislope—1588 to 1607.
Alexander Kinneir, M.A.—1608 to 1654.
Andrew Patersone, M.A.—1658 to 1667.
George Davidson, M.A.—1668 to 1685.
Adam Waddel, M.A.—1685 to 1713.
John Vetch—1715 to 1722.
James Colden—1723 to 1754.
John Waugh—1755 to 1800.
George Drummond—1800 to 1820.
Adam Landels—1821 to 1838.
Robert Cowe, M.A.*—1839 to 1843.
John Robertson—1843 to 1866.
John Alexander Robertson (present incumbent)—1866.

---

shelter—the kirk of Hilton. They had not long remained beneath the sacred roof when the dead man's wound broke out afresh, dripped through the bandages, and was actually lapped by some hounds that had accompanied the procession. For the truth of the tradition we do not vouch. After the Revolution, previously to which he had taken refuge in Holland, Mr Douglas returned to Hilton, and there continued to exercise the pastoral function till his decease at the age of 86.—*New Statistical Account.*

* Cowe was one of those who left the Established Church at the Disruption.

www.ingramcontent.com/pod-product-compliance
Lightning Source LLC
Chambersburg PA
CBHW021814230426
43669CB00008B/745